The Next Three Wars in Israel

Bible Prophecy Now

Arthur Sommerville

Publisher: Ralph Roberts
Editor: Pat Roberts
Cover Design: Ralph Roberts

10 9 8 7 6 5 4 3 2 1

ISBN 1-57090-171-6

The author and publisher have made every effort in the preparation of this book to ensure the accuracy of the information. However, the information in this book is sold without warranty, either express or implied. Neither the author nor **Mountain Church** will be liable for any damages caused or alleged to be caused directly, indirectly, incidentally, or consequentially by the information in this book.

The opinions expressed in this book are solely those of the author and are not necessarily those of **Mountain Church.**

Trademarks: Names of products mentioned in this book known to be a, or suspected of being trademarks or service marks are capitalized. The usage of a trademark or service mark in this book should not be regarded as affecting the validity of any trademark or service mark.

Mountain Church—a division of Creativity, Inc.—is a full–service publisher located at 65 Macedonia Road, Alexander NC 28701. Phone (828) 252–9515, Fax (828) 255–8719. For orders only: 1-800-472-0438. Visa and MasterCard accepted.

This book is also available on the Internet at **abooks.com.** Set your browser to **http:// abooks.com** and enjoy the many fine values available there.

Contents

ACKNOWLEDGEMENTS

I heartily want to thank those who graciously helped us in the writing of this book. David Rowland's research for important information was of particular help. I recognize, too, the hours spent by Miss Laura Copp and my wife in proofreading. I deeply appreciate also the evaluation and suggestions given by Dr. Larry Pearson, pastor of Temple Baptist Church in Anderson, SC. Others have helped by their encouragement and enthusiasm without which it would have been difficult to go on.

DEDICATION

I want to dedicate this book to Irene, my dear wife,
who has stood by my side through many a storm
and has helped me in my ministry for these
past 53 years of our marriage.

PREFACE

The situation in the Near East is heating up daily. The *Jerusalem Post* announced that Security forces are maintaining a high state of alert around the country. There are also plans by terrorists to carry out attacks unprecedented in size and scope and these missions will not all be carried out in Jerusalem. In fact that same newspaper quoted the Chief of General Staff Lt.-General Shaul Mofaz who warned that the Palestinian Authority is preparing for a lengthy conflict, stockpiling weapons and coordinating with the various Islamic groups and Palestinian security services in a unified effort to escalate violence in the region.

Everyone today is wondering if this will lead to the "Big One" or will things just calm down again as they have done so many times during the past 50 years. This book proposes a third scenario that must be seriously considered.

It is not our intention to give a full picture of Bible prophecy. Great men of God have written volumes on this subject and we have built on their foundation. We believe what is accepted and taught in most Bible Schools and seminaries today. We heartily accept dispensational teaching. We will be speaking of the Rapture, the Tribulation Period and the Millennial Age in that order. For those who do not understand this terminology, we will try to simplify it by defining those terms.

In the Apostle Paul's first letter to the church at Thessalonica, chapter 4:13–18 he gives an explanation of what we call the "Rapture." "*But I would not have you to be ignorant, brethren, concerning them which are asleep, that ye sorrow not, even as others which have no hope. For if we believe that Jesus died and rose again, even so them also which sleep in Jesus will God bring with him. For this we say unto you by the word of the Lord, that we which are alive and remain unto the coming of the Lord shall not prevent them which are asleep. For the Lord himself shall descend from heaven with a shout, with the voice of the archangel, and with the trump of God: and the dead in Christ shall rise first: Then we which are alive and remain **shall be caught up together with them in the clouds**, to meet the Lord in the air: and so shall we ever be with the Lord.*

Wherefore comfort one another with these words." The Rapture is that moment when the Lord returns to call all those who have accepted Him as their Saviour and Lord to meet Him in the clouds.

The Great Tribulation is a period of seven years which will follow the Rapture and will be divided into two separate parts of three and a half years each. This period is also called by the term "*Jacob's Trouble*" in the Old Testament, because it will become a terrible ordeal to the Jewish people who will be living at that time. The last part of the seven-year period is also known in the New Testament as the time of "*the wrath to come*" (1 Thessalonians 1:10), for it is in the second half of that Tribulation Period that we see God pouring out His judgments upon the earth.

When we speak of the Millennium, we are talking about the thousand-year reign of Christ when He shall sit on a literal throne and establish His world kingdom of peace. It will be a time when Satan will be bound (Revelation 20:2), a time when there will be no more wars (Micah 4:3) and a time when even the animals will be changed (Isaiah 11:6–8).

What we propose to do in this book is to point out different passages of Scripture we feel have been overlooked in the past and blend them into the scheme proposed above. There will probably be things you have never heard, but we trust that you will consider carefully what is being presented before drawing any conclusions. This book is the fruit of thirty years of study and reflexion. We have preached much of this material before large audiences both in the United States as well as in France and have written articles about it which were printed twenty years ago. We have tried to avoid all sensationalism because that is definitely not the goal of this book. We feel deeply that the events here recorded will be taking place in the very near future and this is the reason we finally decided to go ahead and write this book.

We pray that the thoughts presented in **The Next Three Wars in Israel** will be a blessing to all of you as they have been to us for many years. Most Christians have traveled the big freeways through the prophetic passages of Scripture, but few have gone off on the smaller country roads. Through this book we hope to take you to places you have never seen and allow you to discover verses you never knew existed. Though the events recorded here are not always pleasant, and even sometimes hard to believe and accept, we do want you to receive a blessing as you see God's Hand in everything. His promises are always there to challenge, lead and comfort those who put their full trust in Him.

INTRODUCTION

"Do any of you want to be saved this morning?" This question was asked of all five of us in Henry Sorenson's Sunday school class on that April morning in 1937. In the previous weeks we had been studying prophecy together and learning about the Rapture of the church and the horrors of the Tribulation period that would follow. The Lord had been speaking to me and preparing my heart for this question even before attending that class. I raised my hand immediately and a few minutes later found myself kneeling between my Sunday school teacher and the pastor of the church.

When I asked Christ to enter my heart and life at that moment, He did—and I knew it! I was so filled with joy that I couldn't stay for church but ran all the way home. I remember bursting into the house and shouting, "Mom, I'm saved." She didn't know what I was talking about because no one in our family was saved at that time. However, my mother did open her heart to the Lord a year later, then my grandmother, my brother and finally my father. Praise the Lord, Christ had entered our home and our family was changed.

Since prophecy had played such a big part in my conversion, I remained very interested in it. Three years later, I began my studies at Northwestern Bible School where I had the privilege of sitting at the feet of Dr. Robert Moyer and Dr. W.B. Riley. When I began my studies, I knew more about prophecy than I did about salvation and sanctification! These men impressed upon me the necessity of searching the Scriptures, to seek direction from the Lord for every phase of my life and to preach the Gospel clearly and forcefully. During those four years in school, prophecy was definitely on the back burner and evangelization took its place.

Second World War in the Bible

However, after arriving in Europe in 1946, I saw Germany in rubble and deportation camps all over. It was there I learned of the many things that had happened during the war, as well as of the great decisions taken at Yalta dividing Europe for the end times. My mind turned once again to the great prophetic passages. Could this terrible war we had just witnessed be found somewhere in the Scriptures? The answer to that question had to wait for another thirty years, but finally I found a verse that definitely speaks of the period of World War II.

There is no reference in the Bible to World War I because the Scriptures only relate profane history where the Jewish people are in question, which was not the case at that time. However, we do find the Second World War in the Bible because of the terrible persecution endured under Hitler. In Ezekiel 37 we find that God gave the prophet the vision of the valley of dry bones. We read in verses 9–10, *"Prophesy unto the wind, prophesy, son of man, and say to the wind, Thus saith the Lord GOD; Come from the four winds, O breath, and breathe upon these slain, that they may live. So I prophesied as he commanded me, and the breath came into them, and they lived, and stood up upon their feet, an exceeding great army."* Then from verse 11 through verse 14 God explains that this prophecy has to do with the Jewish people in the end times. *"...whole house of Israel: behold, they say, **Our bones are dried, and our hope is lost**: and we are cut off for our parts."*

This is exactly what the Jews were saying during that terrible Holocaust in Europe. *"Our bones are dried and our hope is lost: and we are cut off ..."* During the Second World War, millions of Jews were being sent to the death chambers; others were being tortured. Families were being divided and all their belongings confiscated. They had no hope whatsoever of being able to return to their homeland, that land that God had promised to Abraham and to his descendants–the land of Israel. (Genesis 17: 6–8) But miracle of miracles–just four years later, on May 14, 1948, Israel was given national recognition by the United Nations as a testimony to all peoples that when God promises something He keeps His Word. He cannot fail.

If our Lord could not keep His Word to Israel, what confidence would we have that He would keep His Word concerning our eternal salvation? All the Bible stands or falls together.

The Psalms also bear witness to the years of the Holocaust. In Psalm 40:12–14 we read, *"For innumerable evils have compassed me about: mine iniquities have taken hold upon me, so that I am not able to look up; they are more than the hairs of mine head: therefore my heart faileth me. Be pleased, O LORD to deliver me: O LORD, make haste to help me. Let them be ashamed and confounded together that seek after my soul to destroy it; let them be driven backward and put to shame that wish me evil."* In Psalm 41:7 we find, *"All that hate me whisper together against me: against me do **they devise my hurt.**"* The German soldiers would ask the Jews as they killed them, "Where is your God now?" Psalm 42:9–10 records, *"I will say unto God my rock, Why hast thou forgotten me? Why go I mourning because of the oppression of the enemy? As with a sword in my bones, **mine enemies reproach me... Where is thy God?"*** And again in Psalm 44:9, 11, 22–23 we read, *"But thou hast cast off, and put us to shame;...Thou hast given us like sheep appointed for meat; and hast scattered us among the heathen...Yea, **for thy sake are we killed all the day long**: we are counted as **sheep for the slaughter**. Awake, why sleepest thou, **O Lord? arise, cast us not off for ever.**"*

God's Promises to His People

In Amos 9:14–15 we read, *"And I will bring again the captivity of my people of Israel, and they shall build the waste cities, and inhabit them; and they shall plant vineyards, and drink the wine thereof; they shall also make gardens, and eat the fruit of them. And I will plant them upon their land, and THEY SHALL NO MORE BE PULLED UP OUT OF THEIR LAND WHICH I HAVE GIVEN THEM, SAITH THE LORD THY GOD."* Here God not only says that He will bring His people back to the land of Israel, but promises them that they shall never be plucked out of that land once they are there. God is protecting them to the extent that if all the nations of the world were to attack Israel, they would not succeed in driving them into the sea.

The Lord goes even farther in His protection of His people as we read in Zechariah 2:4–5 *"Jerusalem shall be inhabited as towns without walls for the multitude of men and cattle therein: For I, saith the LORD, will be unto her a WALL OF FIRE ROUND ABOUT, and will be the glory in the midst of her."* God has hedged in His people with a wall of fire. The same Lord who has given all those promises to Israel is the One who says in John 10:28 *"I give unto them eternal life; and they shall never perish, neither shall any man pluck them out of my hand."* The One who protects Israel is the same One who protects us. The promise of our eternal salvation was given by the same Lord who promised to restore and keep Israel in the last days. Our salvation therefore is linked to Israel and its future. Since His promises to Israel have not failed, nor will they ever fail, we know we can trust Him with our eternal destiny. It is only normal then for all who love the Lord to be interested in what is happening in the Near East these days.

PART ONE: ISRAEL'S FUTURE WARS

And he said, Take heed that ye be not deceived:
for many shall come in my name, saying, I am Christ;
and the time draweth near: go ye not therefore after them.
But when ye shall hear of wars and commotions,
be not terrified: for these things must first come to pass;
but the end is not by and by. Luke 21:8–9

Let not your heart be troubled: ye believe in God,
believe also in me. In my Father's house are many
mansions: if it were not so, I would have told you.
I go to prepare a place for you. And if I go and
prepare a place for you, I will come again,
and receive you unto myself; that where I am,
there ye may be also. John 14:1–3

1

Israel: God's Time Clock

"Ye men of Galilee, why stand ye gazing up into heaven? this same Jesus, which is taken up from you into heaven, shall so come in like manner as ye have seen him go into heaven." (Acts 1:11) These words, spoken by angels, as Christ ascended into heaven became the "living hope" of the disciples. They looked for His coming every day. Something that every true Christian should be doing as he waits for Jesus to return. This "blessed hope" kept the church burning for Christ until the 5th century when Augustine, a Catholic theologian, reasoned that since the Jews were scattered among the nations and no longer had possession of their land which was under the control of the mighty Roman Empire, all the promises of Israel's return to their homeland were not to be considered literally, but should be spiritualized. The word "Israel," in the prophetic books, should be understood to mean "the Church" according to him.

The Birth of Amillennialism

All the promises to Israel, especially the blessings, were now to be applied to the church. Augustine said that Israel could never return to her land–and thus the doctrine of Amillennialism was born. ("A" means "no"–therefore no millennium.) This doctrine teaches that there will be no earthly reign of Christ and claims that we are now in the millennium and Christ is presently reigning. To them it is an invisible kingdom with Christ reigning in the hearts of the believers. This all sounds very spiritual, but for many, it is hard to believe that Satan is now chained, as the Scriptures say he will be during the 1000 year reign of Christ. It is especially hard to believe this when there are Gay Pride demonstrations where more than a million march in favor of homosexuality (as they did in Paris in June 2001). One doesn't see the wolf and the lamb dwelling together nor the cow and the bear feeding beside one another as predicted in Isaiah 11. The Bible predicts a 1000 year reign of peace when Christ shall sit on a literal throne in Jerusalem to reign over the whole earth.

This teaching of Amillennialism became the official teaching of the Catholic Church and has remained so until now. When the great Reformation of the 16th century took place, neither Jean Calvin nor Martin Luther made any change concerning prophecy, but accepted entirely what they had been taught as former Catholics. The official teaching in the Lutheran churches, as well as in all those that come through the teachings of Calvin, still cling to Amillenialism. People stopped looking for the blessed coming of the Lord.

The Rapture Rediscovered

It wasn't until the end of the 19th century that the first "morning star" appeared. John Darby, the English translator of the most accurate of the French Bibles, wrote about dispensations and brought out, for the first time in nearly 1400 years, the blessed truth of the Rapture. At the beginning of the 20th century A.J. Gordon, in Boston, picked up the refrain and published it. This was followed by a multitude of prophetic meetings all over the States. Even the first World War did not stop the great enthusiasm that was building up about the imminent return of Christ, in spite of the fact that a number of preachers began setting dates all of which proved to be false. Christians became more and more convinced that certainly the Rapture must be close as the number of earthquakes multiplied, and famines of unusual dimension were striking one country after another leaving millions dead.

Yes, Christ must be coming soon, but how soon? Where are we on God's Time Clock? To come close to the answer we must look to Israel, God's earthly people. Perhaps there is something hidden in

Scriptures that we might have overlooked which would give us some clue as to just where we fit chronologically into the picture.

Shortly after World War II, Christians, more than ever, began setting dates for the Rapture, feeling that His coming could not be far off. Though everyone sensed the urgency of the hour—could there be a verse that would give us a definite sign that we are very close to His return? It was after we stayed up all night waiting for the results of the vote at the UN building, when the different governments of the world cast their votes as to whether or not to accept Israel as a nation, that a verse came to our minds. Yes, there it was in Isaiah 66:8! *"Who hath heard such a thing? who hath seen such things? Shall the earth be made to bring forth in one day? or shall a nation be born at once?"* In the French version it is brought out a bit clearer where we read, *"Shall a country be brought forth in a day or a nation with one blow."*

On that memorable evening, people all over the world had their ears glued to the radio so as to not miss a single word. As the countries voted, one after another, we could hear first a "yes" and then a "no." The score was tied right to the end. The atmosphere was so tense it could be felt around the world. Then came the last country's turn to declare its intention—and it was "yes." With that one word "yes" the nation of Israel was born. It came into existence literally with *one blow*.

The Last Days

Now, after nearly 2,000 years of silence God had spoken again. At that moment we entered the "last days." We have been in those days now for more than 53 years and we have watched Israel struggle through its first war to gain its independence until today when it is the most powerful nation in the Near East, having its own government, army, schools, hospitals and everything of which modern nations boast today. How can knowing we are in the "last days" help us? First of all, we are no longer basing our conclusions on daily events that catch our attention and make us wonder. It is very true that God is speaking these days and speaking loudly. All nature seems to be against man. Droughts, earthquakes, floods, famines, and tornados have touched the lives of thousands all over the world. This is enough to make us think we are in the last days. Consider, too, how morals are dropping daily. People sinning openly in ways they would never have had the courage to do a few years ago. All this indicates that God's great day of judgment can't be far off, but besides all these deductions, we now KNOW through God's Word that we are in the *"last days."* When, however, will these "last days" come to an end?

Christ Tells Us "When"

When Christ was with His disciples near the end of His ministry, they came to Him with the famous question of "WHEN?" that everyone is asking today. In Mattthew 24:3 we read, *"And as he sat upon the Mount of Olives, the disciples came unto him privately, saying, Tell us, when shall these things be? and what shall be the sign of thy coming, and of the end of the world?"* If we pay close attention to what our Lord answered them, we might come somewhat closer to the answer we so long to know.

After giving His disciples a number of signs that would point to His soon return, He gives them the Parable of the Fig Tree. Before studying this passage in Matthew 24 we must first of all understand the importance of Israel's returning to the "promised land" after so many centuries of being separated from it or of being dominated in it. Theirs was a perilous pilgrimage of unending trials, persecutions and death. We will take the time now to quickly consider the history of the Jewish people to enable us to get a better perspective of what it meant for them to be back in "their land" and witness the "blossoming" of the fig tree after waiting for this event for centuries.

The Event	*Approximate Date*
Egyptian Captivity	1875–1445 B.C.
Assyrian Captivity of Israel (Northern Kingdom)	722 B.C.
1st Babylonian Captivity - Jerusalem (Daniel & Friends)	605 B.C.
2nd Baylonian Captivity 10,000 Jews (Ezekiel)	597 B.C.

3rd Babylonian Captivity   586 B.C.
    Southern Kingdom (Judah)
    First destruction of Jerusalem (9th of AV)

            Jews return in three phases:
1st return   536 B.C.
2nd return   458 B.C.
3rd return   445 B.C.
    (started clock running on Daniel's 490 years)
    Daniel's clock stopped ticking, with 7 years
    remaining, when Christ was crucified in 33 A.D.

Domination by Greece   331–63 B.C.
Domination by Rome   63 B.C.–500 A.D.
Second destruction of Jerusalem   70 A.D.
    Second destruction of the Temple (9th of AV)

        The "Diaspora" (The world-wide dispersion of the Jews)
Byzantines (Persians) controlled Jerusalem   611 A.D.–638 A.D.
Moslems controlled Jerusalem   638 A.D.–1099 A.D.
    Saladin (completed the Dome of the Rock
    mosque on temple site)
Crusaders controlled Jerusalem   1099 A.D.–1187 A.D.
Moslems controlled Jerusalem   1187 A.D.–1291 A.D.
Turks controlled Jerusalem   1291 A.D.–1917 A.D.
British occupation   1917 A.D.–1948 A.D.
Israel back in "her land"   1948 A.D.–
                                              Tribulation Period

The Balfour Declaration was a document signed in 1917 by British Prime Minister Arthur James Balfour after General Allenby and his troops had captured Jerusalem. The Balfour Declaration was a document of British support for creating a Jewish home-land. The Zionist Movement, whose objective was to return the Jews to Palestine, started in the late 1800s because of periodic vio-lence against the Jews in various countries. Leviticus 26:33 *"And I will scatter you among the heathen, and will draw out a sword after you: and **your land shall be desolate**, and your cities waste."*

When the British withdrew from Palestine the United Nations stepped in, partitioned the country and sought to keep the peace. Shortly after, the Jews established the sovereignty of Israel and it was recognized as a nation on May 14, 1948. We cannot help but think of the psalmist when he penned, *"Fear took hold upon them there, and pain, as of a woman in travail....We have thought of thy loving-kindness, O God, in the midst of thy temple....Let mount Zion rejoice, let the daughters of Judah be glad, because of thy judgments."* (Psalm 48:6, 9, 11) These verses express both the pain involved in the birth of Israel as well as the joy of seeing God's intervention on their behalf.

Returning now to the Parable of the Fig Tree, we will see how Christ answers the question of "when?" In this whole 24th chapter of Matthew, Jesus is talking about His return in glory and not about the Rapture. He talks in this parable about the "blooming" of the fig tree, the symbol of Israel. As we have mentioned previously, the fig tree bloomed in May, 1948, when Israel became a nation. Notice, the fig tree bloomed *in our generation* after so many years of waiting. Christ says here that "this" generation, the one that shall see the birth of Israel, shall not pass away before all "these things," (not only the earthquakes, famines, wars and rumours of wars) but also the *"abomination of desolation spoken of by Daniel the prophet, standing in the holy place"* have come to pass.

Let us take a closer look at these signs the Lord has given us:

1. Earthquakes are becoming more and more common: In the 12th century there were but 84 earthquakes, in the 15th century the number increased to 174, in the 18th we find 640 and in the 19th there were 2119. We do not as yet have the figures of the 20th century which will far surpass all the other statistics. God is trying to tell us something.

2. Famines: They are taking on gigantic proportions as millions die yearly in different parts of Africa as well as in the poorer countries of the Orient.

3. Wars: Throughout the world, there have been more than 100 conflagrations since the end of World War II.

4. Sects and False Christs: We see new sects and cults are constantly surging forth and attracting the multitudes. Some offer prosperity under false pretenses and others go farther by pushing their followers to commit mass suicides. Men who hold fast to sound doctrine are becoming almost extinct in this world of confusion in which we live today.

We must also consider the population of the world. In Christ's day there were 300 million; in 1650 there were 600 million; 1.2 billion in 1850; 2.2 billion in 1940 (when I was in high school); 4.8 billion in 1990...and over 6 billion today! The population today is literally exploding!

Added to the population explosion we have the knowledge explosion. Virtually every invention that has modernized our present civilization was invented in the 20th century. This knowledge explosion was predicted by the prophet Daniel 2,500 years ago, *"But thou, O Daniel, shut up the words, and seal the book, even to the time of the end: many shall run to and fro; and **knowledge shall be increased.**"* (Daniel 12:4)

Some Bible scholars decided that the *generation* mentioned in Matthew 24 must be of 40 years duration, because the Israelites spent 40 years in the desert until all of *"that generation"* had died. Calculating from the year 1948, they concluded that Christ would return in 1988. In fact, there was a book written entitled, *Eighty-Eight Reasons Why Christ Will Return In 1988.* When that year passed without the fulfillment of that prediction, others immediately had another explanation by affirming that one must not start counting from the year 1948 but from the year 1967, since that was the year the Jews conquered the old city of Jerusalem. However, wanting to calculate Christ's return by counting 40 years from 1967, they would once again be pin-pointing a specific date which would only prove to be wrong. Christ made it clear that we are not to set dates, for only God Himself knows the day when Christ will return.

Still others continued to cling to the old, more accepted interpretation that the word "generation" refers to the Jewish nation that will never be destroyed, but be preserved to the end times. The problem with this last explanation is that it was superfluous since the Old Testament was filled with passages predicting the return of the Jews to their land and of their preservation in the face of all the nations who would seek their destruction. Christ would not have had to reiterate that fact. But mainly, that explanation would give no answer to the disciples' question of *when* He would return.

Since we entered into the "last days" in 1948, all events recorded in this 24th chapter of Matthew will take place before those who were born that year die off as a generation. At the writing of this book, that generation is only 53 years old and may yet see a good number of years before the last ones die. All who have been born since the formation of the nation of Israel in 1948, form the *last generation.* This *last generation* will be the one that will see the Rapture and the events that will follow it!

All this means that the Rapture is very close and not, as some are beginning to say, perhaps a hundred or two hundred years from now. As soon as Christ had given this parable permitting the disciples to know who would comprise that *generation,* He quickly added *"But of that day and hour knoweth no man, no, not the angels of heaven, but my Father only."* (Matthew 24:36) We are to know the signs that indicate we are close to His coming, but are not to fix a day nor an hour.

Spiritual Discernment

As we wait for our Lord's return we must not overlook a very important warning our Lord gave his disciples. We read in Matthew 16:2–3: *"He answered and said unto them, When it is evening, ye say, It will be fair weather: for the sky is red. And in the morning, It will be foul weather today: for the sky is red and lowring. O ye hypocrites, ye can discern the face of the sky; but can ye not discern the signs of the times?"*

Those who saw and heard our Lord should have had enough discernment, after all that was written in the Old Testament concerning Him, to realize that He was the Son of God manifest in the flesh, the long-awaited Messiah. We will cite some of the prophetic passages concerning Him:

He was born in Bethlehem: *"But thou, Bethlehem Ephratah,* *though thou be little among the thousands of Judah, yet out of thee shall he come forth unto me that is to be ruler in Israel; whose goings forth have been from of old, from everlasting."* (Micah 5:2)

He was born of a virgin: *"Therefore the Lord himself shall give you a sign; Behold, a virgin shall conceive, and bear a son, and shall call his name Immanuel."* (Isaiah 7:14)

He was born of the Tribe of Judah: *"The sceptre shall not depart from Judah, nor a lawgiver from between his feet, until Shiloh come; and unto him shall the gathering of the people be."* (Genesis 49:10)

He was altogether wonderful: *"For unto us a child is born, unto us a son is given: and the government shall be upon his shoulder: and his name shall be called Wonderful, Counsellor, The mighty God, The everlasting Father, The Prince of Peace."* (Isaiah 9:6)

He was without sin: *"Which of you convinceth me of sin?"* (John 8:46)

He spoke with authority: *"And they were astonished at his doctrine: for he taught them as one that had authority, and not as the scribes."* (Mark 1:22)

He commanded the elements: *"And they feared exceedingly, and said one to another, What manner of man is this, that even the wind and the sea obey him?"* (Mark 4:41)

He cast out demons: *"And forthwith Jesus gave them leave. And the unclean spirits went out, and entered into the swine: and the herd ran violently down a steep place into the sea."* (Mark 5:13)

He healed the sick: *"And whithersoever he entered, into villages, or cities, or country, they laid the sick in the streets, and besought him that they might touch if it were but the border of his garment: and as many as touched him were made whole."* (Mark 6:56)

He walked on water: *"And when the disciples saw him walking on the sea, they were troubled, saying, It is a spirit; and they cried out for fear."* (Matthew 14:26)

He forgave sins: *"When Jesus saw their faith, he said unto the sick of the palsy, Son, thy sins be fogiven thee."* (Mark 2:5)

He raised a 12-year-old-girl: *"And he took the damsel by the hand, and said unto her, Talithacumi; which is, being interpreted, Damsel, I say unto thee, arise. And straightway the damsel arose, and walked; for she was of the age of twelve years. And they were astonished with a great astonishment."* (Mark 5:41–42)

He raised a young man: *"And he came and touched the bier: and they that bare him stood still. And he said, Young man, I say unto thee, Arise. And he that was dead sat up, and began to speak. And he delivered him to his mother."* (Luke 7:14–15)

He raised Lazarus: *"And when he thus had spoken, he cried with a loud voice, Lazarus, come forth. And he that was dead came forth, bound hand and foot with graveclothes: and his face was bound about with a napkin. Jesus saith unto them, Loose him, and let him go."* (John 11:43–44)

Moses and the prophets of the Old Testament did great miracles, but no one in the human race, since the days of Adam, ever united so many proofs of Divinity as did this Man. No one ever raised so many from the dead. No one else ever walked on water. No one could ever say, before or after Him, *"which of you convinceth me of sin;"* (John 8:46) Nor could anyone before or after Him ever forgive sins. The Jews of His time recognized this truth, even if millions today think by confessing their sins to a priest they are forgiven. After Christ healed the paralytic He forgave him his sins. We read, *"And the scribes and the Pharisees began to reason, saying, Who is this which speaketh blasphemies?* **Who can forgive sins, but God alone?***"* (Luke 5:21) They were totally right when they said that only God can forgive sins, but their error resided in the fact that they didn't believe Christ was God.

Jesus gave the Jewish people all these signs, and many others, during His lifetime, to show them He was the Son of God But instead of turning to Him as their King, they cried "Crucify Him." They would not accept all the signs and miracles He had been performing before them as proof of His Deity. The Messiah was in their midst, but they failed to recognize Him. They were blinded to the multitude of Scriptures pertaining to Him. This is why He said those stern words: *"O ye hypocrites, ye can discern the face of the sky; but can ye not discern the signs of the times?"* (Matthew 16:3)

But once again we are in Messianic and prophetic times and millions of true believers can't see it, or refuse to believe it. For the past 53 years we have been in the "last days." The existence of Israel today, stands as a visible "sign" that His coming is soon. Scripture passages, lying silent for more than 2,000 years, have been fulfilled before our eyes and yet many remain blinded to them. It is as if we can hear our Lord saying to the Church today, what He said to His disciples 2000 years ago— *"O ye hypocrites, ye can discern the face of the sky; but can ye not discern the signs of the times?"*

2

The Three Wars

As astounding as Israel's birth as a nation has been, the nation's survival in the five wars that have followed its independence is just as miraculous.

1. June 1948, Independence Day until January 7, 1949 - Israel not only survived, but it increased its land possession.

2. October 29, 1956, Israel invaded the Sinai. Overran 40,000 Egyptians, and closed the Suez canal where Israeli ships had been denied passage.

3. June 1967 - The Six Day War - After being attacked, Israel conquered the entire Sinai Peninsula, the Golan Heights in Syria, the territory to the Jordan River, and the old City of Jerusalem.

4. 1973 - The Yom Kippur War - After being once again attacked on the Jewish high holy day (The Day of Pardon), when most Jews were in synagogues or in prayer and fasting. The Arabs' assault was massive and they possessed superior weapons. It was their first technological war. Many Russian weapons had been supplied and the U.S., in return, supplied Israel. There is no explanation for Egypt and Syria not destroying Israel at that time other than by Divine Intervention.

5. June 1982 - Israel invaded Lebanon to destroy the PLO. This was achieved by late September of 1982.

Their land today is thriving. With a population of over 4.5 million people we see a healthy economy based on its agriculture and multiple industries. We shall let the ancient prophet descibe it. Ezekiel 36:35: *"And they shall say, This land that was desolate is become like the garden of Eden; and the waste and desolate and ruined cities are become fenced, and are inhabited."*

Because Israel has already been through five wars since it became a nation, the people do not want to see another one. This is why they are willing to submit to so much terrorism in the hopes it will eventually bring a "lasting peace." Everything was relatively quiet over there until the "Peace Process" was launched and which will probably become the "War Process" before it is over.

How many wars are yet to take place in that small country? When John, the beloved Apostle, was banished to the island of Patmos, the Lord gave him the revelation of the great Battle of Armageddon that will take place in the last days. All students of the Word know about this war because it precedes the coming of the Lord in Glory. However, on closer examination of the Biblical prophecies, we have been brought to believe that there will be three more devastating wars in Israel before the Lord comes to set up His earthly kingdom.

It will all begin with another war between David and Goliath which is prophesied in Zechariah 12. The prophet himself makes the comparison in verse 8 where we read, *"In that day shall the LORD defend the inhabitants of Jerusalem; and he that is feeble among them at that day shall be as **David**; and the house of David shall be as God, as the angel of the Lord before them."* David is pictured here as feeble in the face of the mighty armies that he (representing Israel) will have to confront in the last days. This will be a war between Israel and its closest neighbors, Syria, Egypt and Jordan, for we read, *"In that day will I make the governors of Judah like an hearth of fire among the wood, and like a torch of fire in a sheaf; and they shall devour all the people **round about**, on the right hand and on the left."* (Zechariah 12:6)

Though Egypt has made a peace treaty with Israel, officially Syria and Jordan are still at war with her, even though they are not presently shooting at one another. However, this passage reveals that there will be another war when "David" shall destroy all three of those nations *round about* Israel. Now we shall consider what the Bible predicts concerning each one of these countries of the Near East who will be involved in this coming war.

3

The Israeli-Arab Conflict

SYRIA

"Behold, Damascus is taken away from being a city, and it shall be a ruinous heap." (Isaiah 17:1) This verse seemed to jump right out of the pages of my Bible as I was having my morning devotions. Does this mean that Damascus is going to be totally destroyed? Is this verse for the future or was this prophecy fulfilled in the past? Certainly this verse demanded attention. In the latter days of the kings of Israel, Rezin, king of Syria, and Pekah, king of Israel, decided to besiege Ahaz, king of Judah, but Ahaz called upon Tiglath-pileser, king of Assyria to come to his defense. We then read in II Kings 16:9, *"And the king of Assyria hearkened unto him: for the king of Assyria went up against Damascus and took it, and carried the people of it captive to Kir, and slew Rezin."*

From secular history we learn that when Tiglath-pileser attacked Damascus, only part of the city was destroyed. It never became a ruinous heap and has continued to be inhabited even until now, so this prophecy has yet to be fulfilled! Years later, an article about the city of Damascus, appeared in the *National Geographic Magazine*. Among other things, it said that Damascus is the oldest, continually inhabited city on earth. Other cities could pride themselves to be older, but they were not always inhabited. They had often been destroyed and rebuilt.

The importance of Damascus is seen throughout the whole Old Testament and cited for the first time in relation to Abraham when he returned victorious after going to the defense of his nephew, Lot. This incident occurred when the kings of Sodom and Gomorrah were attacked by Chedorlaomer, the king of Elam along with Tidal, king of nations, Amraphel, king of Shinar, and Arioch, king of Ellasar. (Genesis 14: 1-10). Then in the same chapter, verses 14 and 15, we read: *"And when Abram heard that his brother was taken captive, he armed his trained servants, born in his own house, three hundred and eighteen, and pursued them unto Dan. And he divided himself against them, he and his servants, by night, and smote them, and pursued them unto Hobah, which is on the left hand of **Damascus**."*

Damascus seems to have been properous throughout the centuries that followed and enjoyed a certain amount of God's blessing upon it. It was definitely not the wicked city that Nineveh was. We find the name another time in 2 Kings 8:7–8 when Ben-hadad, the king of Syria, was sick he called upon Elisha, the prophet of God, for help. *"And Elisha came to **Damascus**; and Ben-hadad the king of Syria was sick; and it was told him, saying, The man of God is come hither. And the king said unto Hazael, Take a present in thine hand, and go, meet the man of God, and inquire of the LORD by him, saying, Shall I recover of this disease?"* It is clear from this passsage that Ben-hadad believed in the power of the God of Israel. He believed he could be healed if Elisha, the Lord's prophet, would consent to help him. He sent Hazael, a man of confidence, to seek help. Elisha, on his part, had enough respect for the king that he sent back his answer. *"And Elisha said unto him,* (Hazael) *Go, say unto him, Thou mayest certainly recover: howbeit the LORD hath shewed me that he shall surely die."* (2 Kings 8:10) Elisha knew that Hazael, the messenger that Ben-hadad had sent, would betray and murder him as we read in 2 Kings 8:14–15, *"So he departed from Elisha, and came to his master; who said to him, What said Elisha to thee? And he answered, He told me that thou shouldest surely recover. And it came to pass on the morrow, that he took a thick cloth, and dipped it in water, and spread it on his face, so that he died: and Hazael reigned in his stead."*

It is evident that later in history, the Jewish people must have found a safe haven in the city of Damascus because it was to that city Paul was going to seek out all the Jews there who had accepted Christ as their Saviour and Messiah. It was on his way to

Damascus that he met the Lord and became a disciple. *"And as he journeyed, he came near Damascus: and suddenly there shined round about him a light from heaven: And he fell to the earth, and heard a voice saying unto him, Saul, Saul, why persecutest thou me? And he said, Who art thou, Lord? And the Lord said , I am Jesus whom thou persecutest: it is hard for thee to kick against the pricks."* (Acts 9:3-5) Thus the conversion of the greatest of all the Apostles is closely associated with the city of Damascus.

The Golan Heights

When Israel conquered the Golan Heights, their big guns began shelling the suburbs of Damascus. As one home after another was leveled, we began to wonder if Isaiah 17:1 was about to be fulfilled? Was Damascus going to be totally destroyed now? Moscow wasted no time contacting the White House demanding that the shelling of this city be stopped or the United States would face another world war. Had Israel not stopped its attack on Damascus when it did, only the Lord knows how much other prophecy would have been fulfilled by this time. However, this astounding verse in Isaiah will soon become reality. Damascus will be so destroyed that it will never again be inhabited, but remain forever a heap of rubble!

Syria has seemed to be out of the news for some period of time now, but recently it has found its way back into the media. Everyone feels that no serious breakthrough in the "Peace Process" could ever be obtained unless Israel can settle its differences with Syria. Syria is demanding that Israel restore all the land it occupies on the Golan Heights before considering any future dialogue with her.

A Syrian official recently said that restoring Palestine in its entirety is a long-term goal of Syria. He said this could not be achieved in one stage. The first stage is that of restoring the occupied lands (of 1967) thus guaranteeing the national inalienable right of the Palestinian Arab people. This reveals that Syria's so-called *peace talks* with Israel are only a front for Syria's long-term goal of eventually destroying the nation of Israel.

Syria and Iraq have renewed diplomatic ties that were broken twenty-two years ago when Syria sided with Iran in its war with Iraq. Syria also helped to oust Iraq from Kuwait in the Gulf War of

1991. They are presently joining together to fight a plan by Turkey to build twenty-two dams on the Tigris and Euphrates rivers that would cut off water supplies for Syria and Iraq. Let us not forget that in 1990, Turkey cut off the flow of the Euphrates at its source for thirty days, by creating a huge concrete plug so that a diversion channel could be built and this same act could easily be repeated. (This incident brings to our minds what could happen when the Kings of the East cross that river bed with their 200,000,000 men to confront the Antichrist in the Battle of Armageddon).

Israel, on the other hand, feels it cannot restore all the land it conquered without jeopardizing its security. After Assad was replaced by his son, everyone had hoped that it would be much easier to deal with the situation, but that is not proving to be the case.

In countries such as America, Russia, China and others, their capitals could be bombed out without destroying the whole country. However, in smaller countries, like those of the Near East, the destruction of their capitals is equivalent to the crushing of the whole nation. With the destruction of Damascus, Syria would cease to be a nation, and if Ammon and Cairo were destroyed, Jordan and Egypt would also be brought to their knees. We have seen now how God has predicted the fall of Damascus and with it, the whole country of Syria. But what about Egypt and Jordan?

EGYPT

We find in Isaiah 19:18 a very intriguing verse concerning a city in Egypt. In this verse, we read, *"In that day shall five cities in the land of Egypt speak the language of Canaan, and swear to the LORD of hosts; one shall be called, The city of destruction."* In a conference we held in Paris, before several hundred Jewish people, this verse was cited concerning the future of Israel. Several of them came to me after the meeting to say that in Hebrew that verse really means "The City that was completely destroyed."

To understand what all this means, the verse must be placed in its context. As we read chapter 19, we see that it is talking about the conditions that will exist during the millennial reign of Christ. This is especially clear in verses 23 and 24 where it says, *"In that day shall there be a highway out of Egypt to Assyria, and the Assyrian shall come into Egypt, and the Egyptian into Assyria, and the Egyptians shall serve with the Assyrians. In that day shall Israel be the third with Egypt and with Assyria, even a blessing in the midst of the land."* Only during Christ's great reign of peace could all these blessings take place.

It will be during the millennium that people will talk about "The City of Destruction." We believe it will be destroyed at the same time as Damascus and that the city in question is Cairo, the capital of Egypt.

Why Isn't Cairo Named?

Why doesn't the Bible reveal the name of that city as it did by naming Damascus? The answer is simple—Cairo didn't exist in Isaiah's day. The present city of Cairo (in Arabic: El Kâhira, "The Victorious"), the most populated city in all Africa, is actually the fourth city built on this site and dates from 969. It was founded by Jôhar (Gohar, or Jauhar), the general who conquered Egypt for the Fatimite dynasty of Tunis. Other cities in Egypt that existed then still exist today. Since none of them were mentioned, it is relatively easy to come to the conclusion that the Scriptures here are speaking of that great city of Cairo with its teeming millions.

With the situation in that area of the world being as fragile as it is, peace treaties and pacts can be easily broken. This is particularly true concerning Egypt today. Even as I write this book, there are omens coming out of Egypt that signal a definite change of attitude in Egypt towards Israel. According to reports in the influential Qatar-based as-Jazeera television network as well as in the United Arab Emirates newspaper *al-Bayan*, Cairo intends to stop all diplomatic ties with Israel, restrict the number of Israelis permitted into Egypt and Sinai—a number which has dropped sharply since the the beginning of the recent violence—forbid the buying or selling of Israeli goods and end preferential oil sales to Israel. Though Israel is denying these reports, there is never a considerable amount of smoke without fire. There are more and more antagonists in that country who are protesting against their government's peace treaty with Israel. If the Arab nations were to vote to make war with Israel, Egypt would certainly be among them, and with the destruction of Cairo, all Egypt would fall.

Egypt and The Antichrist

As one considers the events recorded in Daniel 11, it appears that the Antichrist will stretch forth his hand also upon Egypt, for we read in verse 42, *"He shall stretch forth his hand also upon the countries: and the land of Egypt shall not escape."* But there is no mention of him destroying any cities. It only says in verse 43, *"But he shall have power over the treasures of gold and of silver, and over all the precious things of Egypt:..."*

From this verse it would appear that the Antichrist will go to Egypt to seek *"treasures of gold and of silver."* It is while he is seeking treasures in Egypt that he receives word that his adversaries, those "out of the north" and "out of the East" are marching to meet him in that terrible war of Armageddon. (Daniel 11:44)

Egypt played a great role in the Bible from the book of Genesis through to Revelation, being first mentioned in Genesis 12:10, *"And there was a famine in the land: and Abram went down into Egypt to sojourn there; for the famine was grievous in the land."* And the last time the word "Egypt" is used is in Revelation 11:8. *"And their dead bodies shall lie in he street of the great city, which spiritually is called Sodom and Egypt, where also our Lord was crucified."* All in all, the word "Egypt" is mentioned 610 times in Scripture.

Egypt represents the "world" because it was with an "outstetched arm" that God brought his people out of that land to which they were never to return. The word "Egypt" represents sin and the world, to the extent that God linked it with Sodom in that verse in Revelation 11:8 that we just quoted. Then God ties both Sodom and Egypt together to define His city, Jerusalem. This only shows to what extent the "people of God" can fall. This is not only true with His earthly people, but alas, it is often true with His spiritual children. We cannot, in this life, attain a level of spirituality where we are no longer tempted and are able to live totally free from sin. This is why we read in 1 Peter 5:8, *"Be sober, be vigilant; because your adversary the devil, as a roaring lion, walketh about, seeking whom he may devour:"*

The Israelites came out of Egypt, but Egypt didn't "come out of them." They continually longed after the onions and garlic. This is a true picture of Christians today. God calls His children to leave "Egypt" and go to the "promised land," but everyone seems to long after the pleasures they used to experience. It takes a deep work of Calvary in their hearts to tear them away from "Egypt" and create within them a desire for a close walk with the Lord. It is only when one is "weaned" away from "Egypt" that he can finally be free to serve God. The Bible doesn't say that Israel will conquer all of Egypt, but will take land only up to a certain point in the eastern part of that country. Egypt will be an easy prey to the Antichrist.

JORDAN

And now Jordan, the third nation *round about* Jerusalem. Do the scriptures have anything to say about that country in the last days? We must remember that Jordan, as a country, came into being at the end of the First World War, gaining its independence as a hereditary constitutional monarchy in 1946. When the prophets wrote, the area that comprises the Jordan of today was divided into three parts: Edom, Moab and Ammon. In Ezekiel 25:12–14 we read about God's judgment on Edom. *"Thus saith the Lord God; Because that Edom hath dealt against the house of Judah by taking vengeance, and hath greatly offended, and revenged himself upon them; Therefore thus saith the Lord GOD; I will also stretch out mine hand upon Edom, and will cut off man and beast from it; and I will make it desolate from Teman; and they of Dedan shall fall by the sword. And I will lay my vengeance upon Edom by* **the hand of my people** *Israel: and they shall do in Edom according to mine anger and according to my fury; and they shall know my vengeance, saith the Lord GOD."*

In these verses we learn two facts. First of all, we discover that Edom shall become *desolate* and this *by the hand of my people* ISRAEL. Has that already happened or is this a prophecy for the future? This question must always be asked when studying prophetic passages. For instance, a pastor once said that there was no point in looking for an imminent Rapture because according to Ezekiel 29:12, Egypt must be made desolate and the Egyptians scattered for a period of forty years. *"And I will make the land of Egypt desolate in the midst of the countries that are desolate, and her cities among the cities that are laid waste shall be desolate forty years: and I will scatter the Egyptians among the nations, and will disperse them through the countries."* He reasoned that we must wait at least another forty years before Christ could come for His Church because this verse has not been fulfilled as yet.

But upon closer examination of this prophecy we find in the same chapter, verse 19, the explanation. *"Therefore thus saith the Lord GOD; Behold, I will give the land of Egypt unto Nebuchadrezzar king of Babylon; and he shall take her multitutde, and take her spoil, and take her prey; and it shall be the wages for his army."* The prophecy was fulfilled to the letter when Nebuchadrezzar entered Egypt and scattered the Egyptians among the nations for a period of forty years. Profane history records this event when not only the Egyptians suffered, but also the Jews who refused to listen to the prophet Jeremiah who pled with them to remain *in the land,* (Jeremiah 42:15–17). Those Jews went down to Egypt where they were put to death by the armies of Nebuchadrezzar. More details of this invasion are given in Ezekiel 30. No, we don't have to wait another forty years before our Lord can return for His Bride. He can return any day! *"...Even so come Lord Jesus."*

Edom to be destroyed by Israel

Even though it was Ezekiel who told about Egypt being invaded by Nebuchadrezzar as well as his prophecy concerning the destruction of Edom, we cannot draw the conclusion that both of these prophecies have been fulfilled. The differences between the two are great. Ezekiel wrote after Judah and Israel had been taken away from their land. From the year 605 B.C. until May 1948 of our Christian era, Israel never existed as an independent nation nor did it have an army of its own. Egypt was to be invaded by the armies of Babylon, whereas Edom is to be destroyed *by the hand of my people.* Since Israel had no army until our time, this prophecy remains, as of today, unfulfilled.

We have shown that Edom, a part of present Jordan, is to be utterly destroyed *by Israel* in the end days, but what about the other

two countries–Moab and Ammon? For the answer we will go to the prophet Zephaniah 2:9 *"Therefore, as I live, saith the LORD of hosts, the God of Israel, Surely Moab shall be as Sodom, and the children of Ammon as Gomorrah, even the breeding of nettles, and saltpits, and a perpetual desolation: the residue of my people shall spoil them, and the remnant of my people shall possess them."*
Here again we find a scene of utter desolation. Moab and Ammon shall be as Sodom and Gomorrah, totally destroyed by Israel. The devastation is so great it makes us think that this must be the result of a nuclear attack and compares with what we saw in Ezekiel concerning the fate of Edom. Yes, now we have a description of what will happen in the near future in Jordan. In Mathew 24:15–16, Christ is telling His disciples what will happen in the middle of the Tribulation Period. *"When ye therefore shall see the abominatin of desolation...Then let them which be in Judaea flee into the mountains."* Many Bible scholars believe and teach that the Jews, at that time, will flee into the desert in Jordan and hide in the city of Petra, which we believe is the explanation of Psalms 60:9: *"Who will bring me into the strong city? Who will lead me into Edom?"*

Petra

Dr. Jeff Adams, pastor of the Kansas City Baptist Temple, in his recent commentary on the book of Job, brings out a very interesting detail that adds light on this present subject. He, too, teaches that the Jews will flee to Petra in the middle of the Tribulation Period, but adds a detail that is very interesting. I quote now from his book:[1]

> Next we consider the setting of this book, the land of Uz. Like Job's friends, the land of Uz can also trace the origins of its name back to the book of origins, Genesis. *"And the children of Aram; Uz, and Hul, and Gether, and Mash."* (Genesis 10:23) This verse places Uz, for whom the land is named, as a descendant of Shem through Aram. A second mention of Uz is in Genesis 36:28, but this Uz is probably named for the first one. Please note that the context of Genesis 36 connects Edom, Esau and

---

[1] Dr. Jeff Adams, *Job.* Reality Living Publishing, Inc., pages 38–39

Mount Seir, which are all the same. Before the mention of "Uz" in verse 28 we have this statement earlier in the context, *"Thus dwelt Esau in mount Seir: Esau is Edom."* (Genesis 36:8)

A survey of the Old Testament substantiates the claim connecting Uz with Edom. Lamentations 4:21 is clear, *"Rejoice and be glad, O daughter of Edom, that dwellest in the land of Uz; the cup shall also pass through unto thee: thou shalt be drunken, and shalt make thyself naked."*

Uz is also "Idumea," the site of Petra ("rock"), where God will hide his faithful remnant during the last half of the Tribulation. On a map this area is to the southeast and southwest of the Dead Sea, which today would overlap the border between Israel and Jordan.

There has been much talk about "Petra" in recent years, due to the increased awareness of Biblical prophecy. The Biblical foundation for this is God's promise to prepare a place for the faithful remnant in the Tribulation. This place is the place of the "rock."

Earlier we spoke of the prophecy in Revelation 12 where we see that Israel will be persecuted by the Devil in the Tribulation. Let's go back to a verse just before the portion we quoted. *"And the woman fled into the wilderness, where she hath a place prepared of God, that they should feed her there a thousand two hundred and three score days."* (Revelation 12:6) Verse 14 of Revelation 12 is also relevant. *"And to the woman were given two wings of a great eagle, that she might fly into the wilderness, into her place, where she is nourished for a time, and times, and half a time, from the face of the serpent."*

In these verses notice that God has a place prepared for Israel. It is "her place." She is nourished there for a *"time, and times, and half a time,"* which is to say three and a half years the last half of the

Tribulation. Why is she "nourished?" Revelation
13:16–17 tells us that no one could buy or sell without the mark, or the name of the beast. God will
need to nourish this remnant of His people, since
they will not be able to buy or sell.

How will God nourish His people, who have fled
to the place He has prepared for them in the wilderness? Several passages in Biblical prophecy connect
Israel in the coming time of tribulation to Israel in
the time of the exodus. *"Therefore, behold, I will allure
her, and bring her into the wilderness, and speak comfort-
ably unto her. And I will give her vineyards from thence,
and the valley of Achor for a door of hope: and she shall sing
there, as in the days of her youth, and as in the days when
she came up out of the land of Egypt."* (Hosea 2:14–15)

Ezekiel saw the same thing, *"As I live, saith the
Lord GOD, surely with a mighty hand, and with a
stretched out arm, and with fury poured out, will I rule
over you: And I will bring you out from the people, and
will gather you out of the countries wherein ye are scattered, with a mighty hand, and with a stretched out arm,
and with fury poured out. And I will bring you into the
wilderness of the people, and there will I plead with you
face to face. Like as I pleaded with your fathers in the
wilderness of the land of Egypt, so will I plead with you,
saith the Lord GOD. And I will cause you to pass under
the rod, and I will bring you into the bond of the covenant: And I will purge out from among you the rebels,
and them that transgress against me: I will bring them
forth out of the country where they sojourn, and they shall
not enter into the land of Israel: and ye shall know that I
am the LORD."* (Ezekiel 20:33–38)

Again, the connection with the Exodus is in
Micah 7:14–15. Here the element of feeding is
added, and linked with the Exodus. *"Feed thy people
with thy rod, the flock of thine heritage, which dwell soli-
tarily in the wood, in the midst of Carmel: let them feed
in Bashan and Gilead, as in the days of old. According*

*to the days of thy coming out the land of Egypt will I
shew unto him marvelous things."*

We can now understand how this Jewish remnant can survive for three and a half years of Great
Tribulation, when no one will be allowed to buy or
sell without the mark of the beast. God will pro-
vide for them exactly as He did in the Exodus, with
manna from heaven.

What a wonderful thought that God could once again send
manna to feed his people in the desert. But why would the Jews
flee into an enemy country? Why would they even try to find refuge in Jordan? The answer lies in the fact that after the Israeli-
Arab conflict, Jordan will be part of Greater Israel. They will still
be in their own country and there will be no danger there. We
have now seen that all the nations *round about* Jerusalem shall be
destroyed at the hands of the Israeli army, which is one of the
most powerful in the world today.

Nuclear Missiles

After talking to officers in the Israeli army, I found that Israel
has its nuclear missiles directed to the same three cities in the
Arab world with which we have been dealing. Military strategists
have concluded that the next war between Israel and its Arab neighbors would be won or lost in the first 8 minutes. Modern technol-
ogy and warheads of utter destruction are such, that the country
that strikes first will, in all probability, win the war. It is because of
this fact, that the Mossad, Israel's secret service, has agents in
strategic places throughout those three Arab lands as well as in
others. If they learn that a day and an hour has been chosen to strike
Israel, they will, no doubt, launch a pre-emptive strike and destroy
those cities and nations before they can fire their first missile.

Jerusalem Reunited

Long before the War of Independence in 1948, the Jews were
already building a new city of Jerusalem outside the walls of the
old one. The two cities remained completely separated until the

Six-Day War. Until then the Jews had no access to the famous "Wailing Wall" above which stood the Temple in the days of Solomon. When Israel took East Jerusalem, at the end of the Six-Day War, another unusual event took place that momentarily stopped the prophetic clock from ticking for 35 years. On June 1, 1967, feeling assured that Israel was going to win the war over its Arab neighbors, Moshe Dayan was named Minister of Defense, and he, along with the chief of staff, Yitzak Rabin, directed the operations that took their forces to the foot of the Wailing Wall.

Since becoming a nation in 1948, the inhabitants of Jerusalem had never experienced the overwhelming joy that swept over every-one that day when they fully realized they had access to the old city. Now, after so many long years, their beloved Zion, which had been cut off until then, suddenly became one united Jerusalem.

Few people know what happened in the days following that moment. To celebrate this great occasion, the people, carrying banners, marched down the street in front of the wall of Jerusalem. The main banner carried this prophetic text from the Psalms that had been fulfilled before their very eyes just days before: *"I was glad when they said unto me, Let us go into the house of the LORD. Our feet shall stand within thy gates, O Jerusalem. Jerusalem is **builded as a city that is compact together"** (or can also be translated 'the city whose parts have now come together")*. (Psalm 122:1–3) The eyes of the people were opened to see that God had predicted what had happened three thousand years before. If only their spiritual eyes could see and understand what God was predicting in Psalm 22. If only they could see their Messiah as the one who cried out from the cross, *"My God, my God, why hast thou forsaken me."* (Psalm 22:1) It is as if we can hear our Lord crying once more over His beloved city even as He did on Palm Sunday so many years ago: *"Saying, If thou hadst known, even thou, at least in this thy day, the things which belong unto thy peace! but now they are hid from thine eyes."* (Luke 19:42)

In the euphoria of the moment, Moshe Dayan, in a magnanimous gesture to promote a "lasting peace" with the Palestinians and with all the Arab nations, gave control of the Temple Site to the Mufti of Jerusalem, and thus delayed the building of the new Temple for all these years.

The Temple to be Rebuilt

The Bible clearly predicts that the Jews will rebuild the temple before our Lord returns in glory. During the days of the Great Tribulation period, the Antichrist, that man of sin, the son of perdition will desecrate the Temple and proclaim himself God. *"Who opposeth and exalteth himself above all that is called God, or that is worshipped; so that he as God sitteth in the temple of God, shewing himself that he is God."* (2 Thessalonians 2:4) It is evident from this verse and others, that the Antichrist would not be able to sit in the temple unless the Temple were standing in Jerusalem when He comes and breaks his pact with the Jews in the middle of that seven-year period. The Messianic Jews live with a passion to rebuild their temple. Architects have already laid out the plan for its construction. Furnishings have been made for the interior and young men from the Tribe of Levi are presently being prepared to take up their duties in the new temple as soon as it is completed.

To make it even clearer to what extent the Israelis are going in their preparations for the new temple we want to elaborate a bit more on the subject. When the Temple is rebuilt, worship cannot be resumed without the waters of purification produced by the ashes of a red heifer. These waters must be poured over the Temple mount because of the soldiers whose blood has been shed there over the centuries. The recipe for this process must be prepared by a 12-year-old boy who will bring water from the spring Gihon and cast a small amount of ashes on its surface. A hyssop branch will then be used to dip those waters of purification to be sprinkled. This particular boy cannot be born in a hospital (where death has occurred), but must be born in a special home designed to avoid the impurities of the world. The boy must grow up without touching the ground where blood has been spilt or bodies have been buried. There are Jewish women now raising their sons like this because the Messiah is expected soon!

During the last 10 years 500 young Levites have been training for their role as priests in preparation for the resumption of the Temple worship. The Jerusalem Temple Institute has already constructed more than seventy of the Temple vessels and objects which are needed to resume worship.

Why then don't they start building their temple? Because God revealed to David, centuries ago, where the temple must be built, and that directive can never be changed. The problem lies in the fact that on that very site, where the temple must be built, stand two very important mosques dear to the heart of all Arabs in the world. The Israelis would have to destroy those mosques to build their temple and they cannot do that now because world opinion would never permit this, even if they had the courage to destroy them before the eyes of thousands of Arabs. Many hold forth that God will send an earthquake and demolish those two buildings. This, of course, is possible, but we believe that those two mosques will be destroyed during this coming war between Israel and the Arab nations *round about*.

Even with the question of the Temple, we can see again how God has stopped the prophetic clock for these past 35 years. Had Israel not given back the Temple Site to the Arabs, but rather destroyed those mosques during that Six-Day War when they had the opportunity, the Temple would already be standing and this wonderful age of Grace would have ended some time before now. It is evident in our eyes that God is stretching this period of Grace to allow as many as will receive Christ to be saved before the Rapture takes place. Many wonderful Christians fill our churches today who would never have had a chance to be saved had the temple been built years ago! Our Lord is a God of mercy, love...and patience.

A Questionable Verse

Before we can close this section on the Israeli-Arab War there still remains a verse that would seem to suggest that this war we have been explaining, is none other than the War of Armageddon. We refer to Zechariah 12:9, *"And it shall come to pass in that day, that I will seek to destroy **all the nations** that come against Jerusalem."*

In the beginning of this part of the book we cited the 12th chapter of Zechariah as pertaining to the coming war between Israel and the nations *round about* it. From verses one to nine, we see Israel defending itself against the attack from those surrounding nations. In verses 5 and 6 we read, *"And the governors of Judah shall say in their heart, The inhabitants of Jerusalem shall be my strength in the LORD of hosts their God. In that day will I make the governors of Judah like an hearth of fire among the wood, and like a torch of fire in a sheaf; and they shall devour all the people round about, on the right hand and on the left: and Jerusalem shall be inhabited again in her own place, even in Jerusalem."* So we see that Judah will "burn up" their surrounding neighbors as a "fire in a sheaf."

Now we come to Zechariah 12:9, usually thought of as linking the Israeli-Arab Conflict to the Battle of Armageddon because of the expression *"I will seek to destroy **all the nations** that come against Jerusalem,"* whereas in the first verses of the chapter it deals only with the *nations round* about Jerusalem. The verse begins by saying that *"it shall come to pass in **that day**."* The first thought that comes to mind is *that day* must be the same day as in the verses preceeding it. But this is not what it means. The expression *"that day"* refers to any day or event taking place in the "last days." For instance, we read, *"In that day shall there be a great mourning in Jerusalm, as the mourning of Hadadrimmon in the valley of Megiddon."* (Zechariah 12:11) Also in Zechariah 14:8 we read, *"And it shall be **in that day**, that living waters shall go out from Jerusalem; half of them toward the former sea, and half of them toward the hinder sea: in summer and in winter shall it be."*

The situation in the first verses of Zechariah 12 is totally different from what will happen in the Battle of Armageddon where Israel is shown fleeing for her life to the desert. There is no great victory wrought by Israel at the time the Antichrist will invest the land, rifle the houses, rape the women and take half of the city captive, as we find written in Zechariah 14:1–3. Israel will not be like David conquering Goliath in the Battle of Armageddon.

Finally, considering the expression "all the nations" that will come against Jerusalem, it simply means that in the "last days" every nation that will come against Israel will be destroyed; whether it be the "nations round about" Israel, the Russians, or the nations that will march against Israel in the War of Armageddon. Israel is protected by God and no nation in the last days will be able to defeat her.

One more word about this Israeli-Arab conflict is absolutely necessary. It must be clearly understood by everyone that this war will end all enmity between Israel and the Arab nations that has been going on since the days of Abraham. Throughout the whole Millennial Reign of Christ, the Arabs will worship Jehovah, the God of Israel and the Bible and the two nations shall become true brothers in the faith of the same God. Both nations had Abraham as their father, but after the birth of Isaac, Ishmael became a nation whose hand was against his brother and has remained so until this day. The reconciliation of the two nations is recounted in Isaiah 19:24–25 where we read, *"In that day shall Israel be the third with Egypt and with Assyria, **even a blessing** in the midst of the land: Whom the Lord of hosts shall bless, saying, Blessed be Egypt my people, and Assyria the work of my hands, and Israel mine inheritance."*

4

World Persecution

It is a staggering thought to even think of those three cities, Ammon, Damascus and Moab all being destroyed by Israel in the near future, and yet, this is exactly what we have seen as we have walked through those prophetic passages. Just think for a moment what it would mean if an atomic explosion took place over those three cities. More than 20 million people would die in a moment's time. Imagine what would be the impact of all this on world opinion. Even today anti-semitism is gaining ground daily. Cemeteries are being vandalized in various countries and groups are threatening Jewish communities, but—what if 20 million Arabs were killed in a day?

This coming war in the Near East could trigger the greatest persecution of Jews the world has ever seen—even greater than the Holocaust during the Second World War. We read in Jeremiah 16:16 *"Behold, I will send for many fishers, saith the LORD, and they shall fish them; and after will I send for many hunters, and they shall hunt them from every mountain, and from every hill, and out of the holes of the rocks."* Here the Lord is speaking about the Jews being "fished" and "hunted." In those days they fished with a net and thus caught many at a time, but they hunted their game one by one.

At the beginning of this great persecution, many of the Jews will escape to Israel, which at that time will be as the ark was to Noah and his family. It will be the only safe haven (at least for a while) in the entire world. The Jews will be "caught" in the net by the thousands and put to death before they can get to Israel. However, many shall escape to secluded places in the hills and mountains, and there they will be hunted down one by one. In Ezekiel 39:27–28 we find these words, "*When I have brought them again from the people, and gathered them out of their enemies' lands, and am sanctified in them in the sight of many nations; Then they shall know that I am the LORD their God, which caused them to be led into captivity among the heathen: but I have gathered them unto their own land, and have left none of them any more there.*" (Meaning that there will be no Jews in any other land but in Israel)

Can anything be done now to ward off these prophecies from coming to pass? God's Word is sure and these verses will become reality, but this doesn't mean that we shouldn't do everything possible to curtail all anti-semitism wherever it lifts its head. We can also do our best to share our faith with every Israelite we meet. They must know that Jesus Christ not only fulfilled all the prophecies we mentioned above, but many others, such as:

He was betrayed by a friend: "*Yea, mine own familiar friend, in whom I trusted, which did eat of my bread, hath lifted up his heel against me.*" (Psalm 41:9)

He was sold for thirty pieces of silver: "*And I said unto them, If ye think good, give me my price; and if not, forbear. So they weighed for my price thirty pieces of silver.*" (Zechariah 11:12)

He suffered because of our sins: "*But he was wounded for our transgressions, he was bruised for our iniquities: the chastisement of our peace was upon him; and with his stripes we are healed.*" (Isaiah 53:5)

He cried out on the cross the very words that were predicted: "*My God, my God, why hast thou forsaken me?*" (Psalm 22:1)

His garments were parted and lots cast for His cloak: "*They part my garments among them, and cast lots upon my vesture.*" (Psalm 22:18)

His tomb was with the rich: "*And he made his grave with...the rich in his death; because he had done no violence, neiher was any deceit in his mouth.*" (Isaiah 53:9)

He rose from the dead: *"For thou wilt not leave my soul in hell (hades); neither wilt thou suffer thine Holy One to see corruption."* (Psalm 16:10) *"For I know that my Redeemer liveth, and that he shall stand at the latter day upon the earth:"* (Job 19:25)

He ascended into heaven: *"Thou hast ascended on high, thou hast led captivity captive: thou has received gifts for men..."* (Psalm 68:18)

He became High Priest: *"The Lord hath sworn, and will not repent, Thou art a priest for ever after the order of Melchizedek."* (Psalm 110:4)

These, as well as many other wonderful Old Testament prophecies, should be shown to our Jewish friends, for they are ignorant of them. The Jewish people do not learn these truths in their synagogues. They are taught they should never talk with anyone about Jesus. They still stop their ears when this Name, above all other names, is mentioned in their presence. The only message that gets through to them is love. Only love touches their hearts and pricks their curiosity, because they have seen so little of it throughout the centuries. Love makes them wonder why we are different from others.

We must take every opportunity to win God's earthly people to Christ before it is too late. Oh, may hundreds of them, who will eventually have to flee for their lives to the land of Israel, arrive there with full knowledge of how to be saved. May they eventually become the light of that land in the dark hours that lie ahead.

5

The Russian Invasion

What will happen after the Israeli-Arab war and the terrible persecution that will no doubt follow it? Ben Gurion, the first president of Israel, always spoke of "Greater Israel." He saw the boundaries of his country reaching from a Wadi inside Egypt all the way to the Euphrates River. Now, after the Israeli-Arab war, this dream of his will, in all probability, become reality. The peace which they so desire will finally be theirs. The nations *round about* will now be part of greater Israel. However, this long-awaited peace will not last long. There is a formidable enemy already preparing to take the spoil away from Israel—**Russia** with all its allies.

We come now to that prophecy in Ezekiel 38 that has had theologians from around the world studying the magnitude of it. This battle, described with so many details, is called the war of Gog and Magog. This time we do not have to wonder if this war has already taken place or is still in the future. The passage tells us very explicitly that it will take place in the end times for we read in verse 8, *"After many days thou shalt be visited: in the latter years thou shalt come into the land that is brought back from the sword, and is gathered out of many people, against the mountains of Israel, which have been always waste: but it is brought forth out of the nations, and they shall dwell safely all of them."* Only in our days can we say that the Jews have been gathered out of the various nations and are now living among the mountains of Israel. The land, which was nothing but desert when the Jews returned, is now blossoming like a rose. Millions of trees have been planted, fields irrigated and crops reaped as many as three times yearly.

There is only one part of the verse that has not already come true—they are not "dwelling safely" in the land. Violence is everywhere in Israel today. People on both sides are being killed almost daily. All peace efforts end with more bloodshed. This cannot go on forever. In spite of all the attempts by the American government and the leaders of the United Nations, nothing seems to be able to stop another conflict in that area which is definitely in the minds of everyone. We feel that it will be only after this inevitable and devastating war between Israel and the Arab nations that Israel will be finally dwelling in peace and the stage set for the Russian invasion.

Gog and Magog Refers to Russia

We know that Gog and Magog refer to Russia and its allies because verse 6 speaks of them coming from the "*north quarters.*" Russia is the only great country to the north of Israel. Verse 9 says that they shall "*ascend and come like a storm, thou shalt be like a cloud to cover the land, thou, and all thy bands, and many people with thee.*" Ezekiel also names the countries that will be involved in this war: Persia, Ethiopia, Libya, Gomer and Togarmah. (Verses 5 and 6) What is so striking in these verses is the fact that the three *nations round* about Israel, the ones who would be most interested in destroying it, are not even named. Could it be because Syria, Egypt and Jordan will no longer exist as sovereign nations but just part of Greater Israel as a result of the preceding Israeli-Arab War?

Many expositors believe that the word "Meshech" in verse two of this passage refers to Moscow, since the two have the same root meaning. They will be descending "*to take a spoil, and to take a prey;*" and verse 12 goes on to say, "*to turn thine hand upon the desolate places that are now inhabited, and upon the people that are gathered out of the nations, which have gotten cattle and goods, and that dwell in the midst of the land.*" If Israel, at the time of the Russian Invasion, possesses the oil fields of Iraq, the spoil will be even more tempting to Russia. The Bible does not say that Iraq will be taken at the time of the Israeli-Arab War, but we do know that Sadam Hussein will be greatly tempted to get into the act, and will very probably be conquered by Israel at that time.

The War of Gog and Magog is not Armageddon

Many Bible students believe this passage speaks of the Battle of Armageddon, but we see too many differences to link these verses to the Battle of Armageddon recorded in Revelation 19:11–20. John, on the Island of Patmos, saw the Lord descending upon a white horse to deliver His people. We also see that at that same time *"the beast was taken, and with him the false prophet that wrought miracles before him, with which he deceived them which had received the mark of the beast, and them that worshipped his image."* (Revelation 19:20) We find none of these things in Ezekiel 38. We do not see Christ appearing, neither do we see the beast nor his image. The armies of the north are slain by God raining great hailstones upon them, and with an overflowing rain and fire and brimstone, and are not slain by the Lord Himself as He descends to save His people. We read in Revelation 19:21, *"And the remnant were slain with the sword of him that sat upon the horse, which sword proceeded out of his mouth: and all the fowls were filled with their flesh."* The Lord shall slay them by the Word of His mouth, more powerful than any "sword" ever made.

No doubt, the greatest difference between the two wars lies in the fact that when the Russian hordes descend upon Israel, there is a nation or nations which will speak out in the defense of Israel. Look closely at this, *"Sheba and Dedan, and the merchants of Tarshish, with all the young lions thereof, shall say unto thee, Art thou come to take a spoil? hast thou gathered thy company to take a prey? to carry away silver and gold, to take away cattle and goods, to take a great spoil?"* (Ezekiel 38:13). Who are these who speak out against Russia? Some see the expression "the young lions thereof" as referring to the United States since they are the offspring of England. The lion is the symbol of England and America is one of the cubs of the British Commonwealth. It could also be the United Nations or Western Europe who will come to the defense of Israel, but this is not what is most important.

What draws our attention is that there will be a nation or nations who **speak out for Israel** even though they do not go to their defense. It is God Himself who will defend Israel at that time and not some nation or nations willing to go to war with Russia to protect Israel. The Lord says in verse 23 of that same chapter, *"Thus will I magnify myself, and sanctify myself; and I will be known in the eyes of many nations, and they shall know that I am the LORD."* God Himself, defending Israel in such a miraculous way, will definitely be a testimony to the nations that He is still alive and holds the world in His Hand. One would think this tremendous display of His power in the activity of world affairs would bring everyone to their knees and to salvation, but this will not be the case. Men's hearts are cold and indifferent to all that the Lord has done and is doing. No incident, great or small, can bring men to repentance, only the Holy Spirit can soften a heart and prepare it for the entrance of the King of Glory. Another important incident that shows that the war of Gog and Magog and that of Armagedoon are two separate wars is the fact that: **There will be no nation taking the defense of Israel in the War of Armageddon.** Therefore this shows us that the Russian Invasion is the second great war that precedes the coming of our Lord in glory.

The War of Gog and Magog is not that of Revelation 20

One more item must be considered before closing this chapter. In Revelation 20:7–9 we read *"And when the thousand years are expired, Satan shall be loosed out of his prison, And shall go out to deceive the nations which are in the four quarters of the earth, Gog and Magog, to gather them together to battle: the number of whom is as the sand of the sea. And they went up on the breadth of the earth, and compassed the camp of the saints about, and the beloved city: and fire came down from God out of heaven and devoured them."* Here again we find the words "Gog and Magog" mentioned as being a great war at the end time. Is it possible that this one is the same as the one mentioned in Ezekiel 38? Here, all serious Bible scholars are in accord in declaring these two wars are not one and the same.

In Ezekiel 38, the Russian Invasion takes place when Israel shall have returned to its land after being away for a long period of time, whereas in Revelation 20 the war takes place at the end of the thousand-year reign of Christ. Secondly, this later war is led by Satan Himself, since the Antichrist and the False Prophet will already be in the Lake of Fire as recorded in Revelation 19:20 *"And the beast was taken, and with him the false prophet that wrought miracles before him, with which he deceived them that had received the mark of the beast, and them that worshipped his image. These both were cast alive into a lake of fire burning with brimstone."*

Thirdly, this war includes all the "nations which are in the four quarters of the earth" meaning that all peoples will follow Satan to destroy the Holy City of Jerusalem and kill its inhabitants. This is not at all what we see in Ezekiel where the nations that will follow Russia are named. Therefore all the nations of the world are not involved as they will be in this final war.

The outstanding fact that is always present, as we have studied these two great wars, is the Hand of God constantly protecting Israel. God has linked Himself to His promises concerning His people. Through the ages, God has severely judged Israel for her mighty sins, but He stands behind her, ready to come to her defense, when others attack. Notice to what extent He has promised to defend His people, *"For I, saith the LORD, will be unto her a wall of fire round about, and will be the glory in the midst of her."* (Zechariah 2:5) In other words, God is saying here that if all the nations of the world were to unite to attack that small country, wedged between powerful nations and the Mediterranean Sea, they would never be able to defeat Israel. God has put a hedge, a wall of fire around that little country, that no nation or nations will ever be able to penetrate.

As I think of how God's promises surround Israel, I praise Him that He has also surrounded us with mighty promises. I love to think of the one found at the end of Paul's letter to the church at Rome, *"Nay, in all these things we are more than conquerors through him that loved us. For I am persuaded, that neither death, nor life, nor angels, nor principalities, nor powers, nor things present, nor things to come, nor height, nor depth, nor any other creature, shall be able to separate us from the love of God, which is in Christ Jesus our Lord."* (Romans 8: 37–39)

6

The Battle of Armageddon

We come now to the third and last battle that comes at the end of the Great Tribulation period. This war is much better known than the two we have just studied. Since so many books have been written regarding this last war, we shall just make a few remarks before leaving this subject.

The First Part of Armageddon

It is very clear as we read Revelation 19:11–16 that there will be a great war in Israel when the heavens will open and Christ will appear, seated on a white horse to judge and make war. Another description of this war was given to us in Revelation 14:14–20. This great war, Armageddon, the greatest one of all times, will be held in a valley located 18 miles southeast of Haifa at the edge of the city of Megiddo. Its strategic location at the crossing of two military and trade routes gave this city an importance far beyond its size. It was in this very valley that Josiah, the King of Judah, died while opposing the advance of the Egyptian King Neco II, who was marching towards Assyria. Other Old Testament wars also took place on that very location. The valley is flat and offers an excellent field for maneuvering. The valley is so big that Napoleon, standing on a rock near the city of Megiddo, said that there was enough room in that valley to hold all the armies of the world.

The word "Armageddon" derives its name from the city of Megiddo because "Har" means "hill" in Hebrew and so it is the

"Hill of Megiddo." The Bible presents this conflict in two parts. In the first half we see the the armies of the North and those of the East coming to make war against the Antichrist, as mentioned in Daniel 11:44. According to Revelation 9:16 there will be 200,000,000 men coming from the East, for we read: *"And the number of the army of the horsemen were two hundred thousand thousand:"* Verse 14 of the same chapter mentions the Euphrates River and in Rev. 16:12 we are given more light about this river when we read that *"the water thereof was dried up, that the way of the kings of the East might be prepared."*

The only country in the world today that can raise an army of that magnitude is China. No one can imagine witnessing an army of 200 million horsemen and soldiers coming across a dry river bed. The image of this was engraved so deeply in the hearts and minds of the Armenian people, that for centuries, when they would meet each other they would ask, "Is the Euphrates dried up?" They lived in constant fear of the Chinese hordes coming upon them.

Then we must consider the great army coming out of the North. They too will number into the millions and will all battle against the Antichrist and his armies in that infamous valley of Armageddon, mentioned by name in Rev. 16:16. It is therefore evident that though a great many soldiers will die on the mountains of Israel in the battle of Gog and Magog, Russia will again be able to raise a formidable force to make battle against the Antichrist. This war is clearly pictured for us in Joel 3:12–16: *"Let the heathen be wakened, and come up to the valley of Jehoshaphat:* (another name for that same valley of Jezreel–the valley of Armageddon) *for there will I sit to judge all the heathen round about. Put ye in the sickle, for the harvest is ripe: come, get you down; for the press is full, the vats overflow; for their wickedness is great. Multitudes, multitudes in the valley of decision: for the day of the LORD is near in the valley of decision. The sun and the moon shall be darkened, and the stars shall withdraw their shining. The LORD also shall roar out of Zion, and utter his voice from Jerusalem; and the heavens and the earth shall shake: but the LORD will be the hope of his people and the strength of the children of Israel."*

All this coincides with what we read in Revelation 14:19–20 *"And the angel thrust in his sickle into the earth, and gathered the vine of the earth, and cast it into the great winepress of the wrath of God. And the winepress was trodden without the city, and blood came out of the winepress, even unto the horse bridles, by the space of a thousand and six hundred furlongs."* That valley of death, that great *"winepress of the wrath of God,"* which measures 32 miles long and 6 miles wide will be covered with blood to the depth of a horse's bridle!

When I had the privilege of visiting Israel the first time, nothing so impressed me, apart from Calvary and the Tomb, as this great valley, stretching out before our eyes totally covered with its crops waving in the wind. As our bus made its way toward the town of Nazareth, I couldn't help but think, as I dried the tears from my eyes, someday in the near future, this whole stretch of land will be covered with blood to the depth of four feet or more!

The Antichrist will come forth victorious from this horrendous conflict as the absolute ruler of the earth. He will have, for a short time, all that Satan promised Christ when he took Him to a high mountain and showed Him *"all the kingdoms of the world, and the glory of them; And saith unto Him, All these things will I give thee, if thou wilt fall down and worship me."* (Matthew 4:8–9) Satan still offers earthly honor and glory to all who are ready to bow down and worship him, but what will be true of the Antichrist will also be true of everyone who listens to Satan today—their reign in sin will be short and their eternal loss will be the horrible consequences that will follow. No one ever wins with Satan.

The Second Part of Armageddon

Now comes the second part of the war of Armageddon. Antichrist, proud of his great victory over the nations, will be moved by Satan to put an end to the nation of Israel and to all the promises God has made to that people. He will, once again, try to prove God a liar and unable to keep His promises. By so doing, he hopes to make God a sinner and thus incapable of judging him or anyone else. This has been his goal throughout all of time.

The Jews who will have found refuge in their land are now to be pushed into the sea and destroyed. The Antichrist will march directly south to the city of Jerusalem and the description of what will happen at that time is recorded in Zechariah 14:2–4. He will enter Jerusalem, *"the city shall be taken, and the houses rifled, and the women ravished; and half of the city shall go forth into captivity...Then shall the LORD go forth, and fight against those nations, as when He fought in the day of battle."*

The Lord Himself does not enter into the fray until His people are threatened with total destruction. It is at this time that John, on the isle of Patmos, records his vision in the book of Revelation 19:11–16: *"And I saw heaven opened, and behold a white horse; and he that sat upon him was called Faithful and True...And he was clothed with a vesture dipped in blood: and his name is called The Word of God. And the armies which were in heaven followed him upon white horses, clothed in fine linen...And out of His mouth goeth a sharp sword, that with it he should smite the nations: and he shall rule them with a rod of iron: and he treadeth the winepress of the fierceness and wrath of Almighty God. And he hath on his vesture and on his thigh a name written, KING OF KINGS, AND LORD OF LORDS."*

The great battle is now over and our Lord is the mighty Conqueror and King and He shall reign on this earth for a thousand years. No, we are not in the Millennium yet, but we soon shall be. We will know we are in Christ's thousand-year reign when we shall see Him on His throne in Jerusalem.

7

The Time Factor

We know that the Battle of Armageddon will take place just prior to the return of the Lord, but when will the Israeli-Arab war and the Russian Invasion take place? Neither of these two conflicts are even mentioned in Revelation which deals with the events that will take place during the Tribulation Period. Must these two wars take place before the Rapture? These and other questions need to be answered before we can leave this subject of the three wars that precede the return of our Lord in glory.

First of all, we must keep in mind that our Lord's coming is imminent and there is nothing hindering Him from rapturing His Church at any moment. This is the "Blessed Hope" that has been given to every believer. This is the hope that has kept God's children rejoicing throughout this whole Church Age. We must look for His coming daily and keep our lamps shining brightly.

This having been said, we must still find an answer to the question of when these two wars will take place. It has always been taught and believed that the Tribulation Period will follow this wonderful Age of Grace—and we firmly believe that it will. However, those who believe this, declare that it will occur immediately after the Rapture. Without saying it in so many words, many conclude that the Antichrist will begin his reign *the day after the Rapture*. But this is not what the Bible teaches.

When Does the Great Period of the Tribulation Begin?

Daniel, in chapter 9 verse 27, tells us *exactly* when the Tribultion Period will begin: *"And he shall confirm the covenant with many for one week: and in the midst of the week he shall cause the sacrifice and the oblation to cease..."* Here, Daniel is saying that the Antichrist shall make a covenant with the government of Israel for seven years (one week) and after three and a half years he shall break that covenant. This coincides perfectly with what we read in Matthew 24:15-16, *"When ye therefore shall see the abomination of desolation, spoken of by Daniel the prophet, stand in the holy place, (whoso readeth, let him understand:) Then let them which be in Judaea, flee into the mountains."* The "holy place" where his statue shall be erected is at the Temple in Jerusalem. The Beast will desecrate the Temple and break his pact with Israel in the middle of the "week," or in the midst of the seven-year covenant.

We learn much about the coming of our Lord from the 24th chapter of Matthew. We must never forget, while reading this chapter, that the signs that are given there deal with our Lord's Second Advent, and not the Rapture. The Rapture shall have already taken place when everyone shall see the "abomination of desolation" mentioned above. Most Christians miss the mark when reading the words, *"Then shall two be in the field; the one shall be taken, and the other left. Two women shall be grinding at the mill; the one shall be taken, and the other left."* Most people apply Verses 40 and 41 to the Rapture. These verses picture exactly what will take place at that time, but this is only an illustration of that event and not the explanation. We must constantly remember to seek out the explanation of a passage before using it as an illustration.

These verses were used by our Lord to describe what will happen at the end of the Tribulation Period, just before the return of our Lord in Glory. They are not a description of what will happen at the time of the Rapture, even if that would seem to be the logical explanation. The key lies in the earlier verse, where we read, *"But as the days of Noe were, so shall also the coming of the Son of man be."* (Matthew 24:37) At the time of the great flood in the days of Noah, those who were *"taken"* were drowned in the waters that covered the earth and those who were *"left"* were Noah and his family to enter into a new era. So shall it be when our Lord returns in His Second Advent. In Matthew 13:49–50 our Lord says, *"So shall it be at the end of the world: the angels shall come forth, and sever the wicked from among the just, and shall cast them into the furnace of fire; there shall be wailing and gnashing of teeth."* So we see clearly stated here that those who "will be taken" will be snatched away by the Angels and cast into Hell, whereas, those who "will be left" will be permitted to enter into a new era—the wonderful Millennium age.

Is The Rapture in Matthew 24?

An evangelist friend of mine was driving us home late one evening when "out of the blue" he asked me, "Do you think the Rapture will take place at the end of verse 12 in Matthew 24." I was almost asleep when he spoke and wondered if I had really heard what he was saying. Naturally, I asked him to repeat the question and when I fully understood, I was at a total loss to give him an answer. I hadn't memorized that chapter and didn't know what happened at verse 12, nor why he had chosen that verse in particular. The question, however, had not fallen on deaf ears and in the days following I considered seriously what he had asked me. Since I knew that Christ was not talking about the Rapture in that chapter, my first reaction was just to dismiss the question altogether. But not being satisfied with my conclusion, once again I began to think about the passage. Was Christ refering to the Rapture when He gave those first verses in that chapter? And is there a serious break between verses 12 and 13?

I realized then, for the first time, that everything seems to change in the chapter. The verses preceding verse 12 are actually taking place today, but from then on, it is clear that all the following ones deal only with the Tribulation Period. Verse 13 places salvation on a conditional basis. Only those *"who endure to the end shall be saved"* because during the terrible period that will follow the Age of Grace, those who believe in Christ are not *"sealed with the Holy Spirit till the day of redemption"* (Ephesians 4:30) as is true today, but live under a *condition.* The Tribulation saints must strive to keep their salvation. This does not mean that they would lose it because of the some *lust of the flesh*, a *lust of the eyes*, or the *pride of life* but rather the *condition* will depend upon their continuing to refuse the mark of the Beast even until death. *"And I saw thrones, and they sat upon them, and judgment was given unto them: and I saw the souls of them that were beheaded for the witness of Jesus, and for the word of God, and which had not worshipped the beast, neither his image, neither had received his mark upon their foreheads, or in their hands; and they lived and reigned with Christ a thousand years."* (Revelation 20:4)

This situation does not exist at this time. We are given "eternal life" when we accept Christ, and "eternal life" means that when Christ saves us we are saved forever, and not just for a limited time depending on our faithfulness or good works. Christ will not rapture a mutilated "body" which would be the case if we could lose our salvation. We have been *sealed* with the Holy Spirit as a mark of our belonging to Christ for eternity.

Those signs in the first verses of Matthew 24, have to do with wars, famines, pestilences, earthquakes and false prophets; signs that people living under the rule of the Antichrist will not need to be persuaded that they are living in the days just preceding the coming of the Lord. These are, however, signs we are witnessing today to show us His return in glory is not far off, and the Rapture will come even sooner! These signs are more evident every day as we witness catastrophe after catastrophe. God is speaking loudly, but the world is not listening. The Trump of God can sound at any time but people go on as if they were going to live forever and never stand in judgment before God, who is a *consuming fire.*

The day after the Rapture, the whole world will be in utter confusion and turmoil. Everyone will be wondering and talking about the millions who are missing. The media will try to bring some "logical" explanantion of what has happened. Many will explain the dsappearances by saying that those who were missing simply went back to their "home," since they were aliens and not of this world. There has been such a great multiplication of films about aliens and testimonies of people who claim to have seen beings from another planet, that it will seem perfectly natural to accept that assumption. This explanation will satisfy the untold millions of unsaved who had no close relationship to a true child of God, but this explanation will not satisfy those who had children or parents who had witnessed to them hundreds of times and had even told them that one day they could be taken out of this world to meet their Lord in glory. However, they will be in a strict minority and their voices will fail to persuade anyone to the contrary.

The Rapture will certainly be the cause of many accidents, both on the road and in the skies, as drivers and pilots are caught away. Weeks will pass before things will even begin to settle down to normal. The Man of Sin, spoken of in 2 Thessalonians 2 will not be known to the world until after the Rapture, *"For the mystery of iniquity doth already work: only he* (the Holy Spirit) *who now letteth will let, until he be taken out of the way. And then shall that Wicked be revealed, whom the Lord shall consume with the spirit of his mouth, and shall destroy with the brightness of his coming."* (2 Thessalonians 2:7–8) Here Paul is saying that the Holy Spirit, working through the church, will hinder the work of Satan until the day the Church is raptured...and *then* shall the Antichrist reveal himself.

Who Is The Antichrist?

In spite of this verse, which states clearly that the Antichrist will not be known until after the Rapture, that has not stopped people from trying to guess who he might be. In the 1940s, Hitler, Mussolini and Stalin were all mentioned as candidates. The Pope has been the choice of millions ever since the Middle Ages. Many believe firmly that whoever he is, he will be an Israelite. Though the Lord never revealed the name of the Man of Sin, He did tell us in several places in Scripture that he will be an Assyrian. In Isaiah 14:25, we read: *"That I will break the **Assyrian** in my land, and **upon my mountains** tread him under foot: then shall his yoke depart from off them, and his burden depart from off their shoulders."* It could be said that this verse applies to Nebuchadnezzar, but he died in Babylon and was not broken by God on the mountains of Israel and the burden did not depart from the shoulders of the Jewish people after that monarch died.

The Lord makes it clear that the Assyrian is the Antichrist in Isaiah 31:8, *"Then shall the Assyrian fall with the sword, not of a mighty man; and the sword, not of a mean man, shall devour him."* In the

French translation the verse is even clearer where we read, *"And the Assyrian shall fall under a sword which is **not that of a man**, and the sword which is **not that of a man** shall devour him."* This verse makes it clear that the Antichrist shall be slain by the sword of the Lord.

However, making it still clearer, we have that wonderful Christmas passage found in chapter 5 of the book of the prophet Micah where we read those well-known verses concerning the birth of our Lord. We find in verse 5, *"And this man* (the One who is to 'come forth to be the ruler in Israel: whose goings forth have been from of old, from everlasting' verse 2) *shall be the peace,* (or bring the peace) *when the Assyrian shall come into our land."* The Assyrian, the Antichrist, shall invade the land of Israel, and then shall the Lord appear to defend Israel and bring everlasting peace to the land as we read in Zechariah 14:2–4 *"For I will gather all nations against Jerusalem to battle; and the city shall be taken, and the houses rifled, and the women ravished; and half of the city shall go forth into captivity, and the residue of the people shall not be cut off from the city. Then shall the LORD go forth, and fight against those nations, as when he fought in the day of battle. And his feet shall stand in that day upon the mount of Olives, which is before Jerusalem on the east, and the mount of Olives shall cleave in the midst thereof toward the east and toward the west..."*

Who Are The Assyrians?

It is very easy for many to confuse the Assyrians with the Syrians. These are two separate peoples who lived in two different parts of the Near East. The Assyrian Empire was located in the Mesopotamian Valley and had Nineveh as its capital. The first reference to Nineveh in cuneiform texts is that of Shamshi-Adad I, who ruled Assyria in the 18th century B.C. However, it wasn't until the reign of Sennacherib (704-681 B.C.) that it attained its glory as the capital of the the Assyrian Empire. It existed before the Babylonian Empire. It was situated on the east bank of the Tigris opposite the Modern city of Mosul in northern Iraq (Upper Mesopotamia). The Assyrians were extremely wicked, to the extent that they would skin alive their captives or bury them alive. Their sexual orgies went beyond anything one could imagine. They were extremely powerful and ruled over many peoples at that time. It was to that wicked city, Israel's dreaded enemy, that God sent His servant Jonah to tell them that in forty days Nineveh would be destroyed.

God brought great conviction of sin to all the inhabitants, including the king, for we read: *"For word came unto the king of Nineveh, and he arose from his throne, and he laid his robe from him, and covered him with sackcloth, and sat in ashes. And he caused it to be proclaimed and published through Nineveh by the decree of the king and his nobles, saying, Let neither man nor beast, herd nor flock, taste any thing: let them not feed, nor drink water: But let man and beast be covered with sackcloth, and cry mightily unto God: yea, let them turn every one from his evil way, and from the violence that is in their hands. Who can tell if God will turn and repent, and turn away from his fierce anger, that we perish not? And God saw their works, that they turned from their evil way: and God repented of the evil, that he had said that he would do unto them, and he did it not."* (Jonah 3:6–10)

Their turning from sin was a veritable revival. God had brought a miracle into their midst. Unhappily, this great work of God didn't last. This is not an isolated case. How many times churches today, and even entire countries, have experienced a great moving of the Holy Spirit in their midst, but after a few years, and sometimes only a few weeks, people return to their old ways and the revival would end. We saw that happen in Wales after their great revival. We saw it take place in the United States following the great revival that began in New York City and swept across the whole country. Revivals are hard come by, but the continuation of them is even harder.

One hundred and fify years after the preaching of Jonah, God sent them another prophet, Nahum, but this time it was only to announce the coming judgment of God upon them because they were, once again, deep in their past sins. Listen to the message in Nahum 1:2, *"God is jealous, and the LORD revengeth; the LORD revengeth and is furious; the LORD will take vengeance on his adversaries, and he reserveth wrath for his enemies."* And again in chapter 3, *"Woe to the bloody city! it is all full of lies and robbery; the prey departeth not; the noise of a whip, and the noise of the rattling of the wheels, and of the prancing horses, and of the jumping chariots. The horseman lifteth up both the bright sword and the glittering spear: and there is a multitude of slain, and a great number of carcases; and there is none end of their corpses; they stumble upon their corpses: Because of the multitude of the whoredoms of the wellfavoured harlot, the mistress of witchcrafts, that selleth nations through her whoredoms, and families through her witchcrafts. Behold, I am against thee, saith the LORD of hosts; and I will discover thy skirts upon thy face, and I will shew the nations thy nakedness and the kingdoms thy shame."* (Nahum 3:1-5)

The judgment of God came swiftly. It was awesome. It fell in 612 B.C. under the combined attack of the Medes and the Babylonians. Somehow or other, the city ended up by being totally buried. For centuries kings and armies marched over the place, never realizing that under their feet was buried the ancient city of Nineveh. In the ensuing centuries no one even knew where that ancient capital was located. In fact, for years scholars doubted the city ever existed and riduculed the two prophets, Jonah and Nahum who wrote about it. The world had to wait until the nineteenth century before archeologists discovered and unearthed parts of this buried metropolis.

All Assyrians were not in Nineveh when God buried it. There are still Assyrians in Iraq today. They live in the northern part of that country separated largely from the rest of the population. They are not Arabs and their religion is very occult and Satanic. This Man of Sin could have been born in that area of the world or even in a Western Nation. (There is a town in southern France where many of its inhabitants are Assyrians, but who blend in completely with the French. No one would ever detect their real identity.) It is very probable that The Man of Sin would attend some important university in Europe or in the United States. In any case, he will be extremely intelligent and endued with extraordinary power.

This answers the question about the possibility of the Man of Sin being an Israelite. Revelation 13:1 speaks about the Beast rising up out of the sea. The "sea" in Scriptures refer to the nations, and even though the Beast, mentioned in this passage, speaks of a ten-nation confederacy in the end times, it also speaks of a man, the Antichrist. *"And I saw one of his heads as it were wounded to death; and his deadly wound was healed: and all the world wondered after the beast. And they worshipped the dragon which gave power unto the beast: and **they worshipped the beast**, saying, Who is like unto the beast? who is able to make war with him?"* (Revelation

13:3–4) These verses present a "man" and not a confederacy of nations because men don't worship a government; they would only worship a person. He will demand this adoration even as did the great monarachs of the past. The verse asks the question, "*Who is able to make war with him?*" (meaning, who is able to make war with the Antichrist). And the answer is the Lord Jesus Christ, who will slay him with a Word from his mouth.

The false prophet is spoken of as coming from the *land.* "*And I beheld another beast coming up out of the earth.*" (Revelation 13:11) When the writer mentions the earth (land), he's talking about the land of Israel. The false prophet will, no doubt, be an Israelite, and this fact will help the Antichrist to win the confidence of the Jews in Israel to make a pact with the new world leader. Since we are so close to the coming of the Lord, it is very easy to assume that both the Antichrist and the False Prophet are presently alive somewhere in the world and waiting for the moment when they will be allowed to disclose their identity.

The Pyramid

Even with all his gifts and power it is evident that The Man of Sin could never, the very next day, be able to make a peace pact with Israel. It will definitely take some time for him, totally unknown before the Rapture, to become head of a world government. However, that would not be his greatest challenge since there is already a "pyramid" of men and women waiting for the *Capstone* to come and take over. (The pyramid is becoming more and more the symbol of the "New World Order.") This term was coined by former President George Bush just before he ran for his second term against President Bill Clinton. After those elections, the term slipped out of usage. However, now we are hearing the expression again. It is being used to describe the readjusting of the entire missile program between America and Russia to cope with a new situation brought about by President George W. Bush deciding to go ahead with his anti-ballistic missile program.

What do they mean by the term "The New World Order?" They want to present to everyone all the advantages there would be to have no more borders, one currency, an accepted world religion and a government strong enough to bring order, where today we only find chaos, violence and wars. It is a promise that with a "world government," life would be made easier for everyone and prosperity wouldn't be the privilege of just a selected "elite."

However, when one looks carefully at the "bottom line", the situation is exactly the opposite. The rich would become richer and take control of everything and the poor would become poorer. We are talking about a world-wide dictatorship. The freedoms that we presently enjoy would be taken away. A system monitoring the whereabouts of everyone (which, by the way, already exists) would be forced on all as the new way of life. It would completely prevent anyone from trying to worship elsewhere than in places designated by the world government. No one would be able to strike for higher wages or manifest their disapproval of the actions of the new men in power. "Accept what is told you and shut up" would be the new order of the day. Many other scenarios could be described, but we believe this is sufficient to paint the picture.

When François Mitterand became President of France, he ordered the construction of a pyramid to be the only entrance to the most prestigious art gallery of the world, the Louvre. Not only that, but he also asked the Japanese architect to make it out of 666 panes of glass—and he did! Everyone visiting the Louvre must walk under that pryramid. Now, when one enters the Louvre he not only passes under a pyramid, the symbol of Satan, but also under the number 666 which is the number of the Beast. By doing this, Satanists believe that in some way, they have already placed people under a Satanic influence and thus making them more ready to accept new anti-God measures. The leftist mayor of Lille, a city in northern France, had pyramids placed over the entrance of every subway station in that metropolis of a million people!

These men are doing all in their power to set up a one-world government and a one-world religion. Much could be written about this "machine," as I have nicknamed this powerful organization comprising the great fortunes of this world known as the "establishment," but also including political leaders, religious figures, journalists, the Mafia, etc. However, that is not our goal at this time.

The efforts of the Antichrist to persuade Israel to sign a covenant with him will be slowed down because he will first have to gain their trust in him and in his "new world order" enough to sign this "pact." Let us not forget that prior to the revelation of the Antichrist, the Jews will have gone through great persecution throughout the whole world and that hatred will have been greatly built up between Israel and the other nations. How long will it take for the Antichrist to come to power and win the confidence of the leaders of Israel to the extent that they will be willing to sign a pact?

Though we cannot fix a definite time table between the Rapture and the Great Tribulation, we do know that there will be a period separating the two, which we will call the "interval." It is in this time frame that the first two wars could take place, since there is no mention of either of them in the book of Revelation. It would be logical to assume that the Russian Invasion will take place during the "interval," but we cannot say the same about the Israeli-Arab War, which could take place even before this book is printed. The situation is constantly deteriorating. Just what it will take to blow up the whole Near East is still not known, but we definitely feel it is not far off. If the Church is still here to witness the Israeli-Arab conflict...and if it is still here to see the destruction of the mosques...and also the great persecution of the Jews, will it still need more proof that the Rapture is close? What will it take to open the eyes of Christians today? It seems we can almost hear the Trump of God. Are we really ready for our Lord's imminent return? Have we done what He asked us to do? Have we *invested* our lives and money in eternity? How much greater will be the eternal dividends on money invested in God's work now! It is much more secure in the Bank of Heaven than invested in stocks and bonds which rise and fall daily leaving many people bankrupt.

The Lord has promised a crown for those who love His appearing. We already have enough proof and signs that His coming is near that we should live every day of our lives for His glory. The things of this earth should begin to fade before our eyes as we contemplate the fact that we shall soon be with Him forever. Are you ready to meet Him today?

PART TWO: BABYLON THE GREAT

Babylon is suddenly fallen and destroyed.
(Jeremiah 51:8)

And Babylon shall become heaps, a dwellingplace
for dragons, an astonishment, and an hissing,
without an inhabitant. (Jeremiah 51:37)

Babylon the Great

There in front of my eyes, as I stood waiting for my train in a small town in Slovakia in 1946, was a big poster revealing a beautiful view of the skyline of New York with this inscription written above it "THE GREAT CITY." Remembering that this very term is used concerning the woman who represents Babylon in Revelation 17:18 where we read, "*And the woman which thou sawest is that great city, which reigneth over the kings of the earth.*" Could the "Big Apple" be Babylon the Great? "No, of course not, Rome is Babylon" I said to myself, "Everyone knows that." And immediately put the whole thing out of my mind.

Many books have been written about ancient Babylon as well as about how the name is applied to a city in Revelation. In Hebrew the word Babylon is BAVEL, or BABEL, and in Arabic ATLAL BABIL. It is one of the most famous cities of antiquity. It was the capital of southern Mesopotamia (Babylonia) from the early 2nd millennium to the early 1st millennium B.C., and capital of the Neo-Babylonian (Chaldean) Empire in the 7th and 6th centuries B.C., when it was at the height of its spendor. Its extensive ruins on the Euphrates River, about 55 miles south of Bagdad, lie near the modern town of al-Hillah, Iraq.

Christians associate the word Babylon with Nebuchadnezzar who was the first great monarch of that city. When Daniel explained the king's dream, he told the monarch that he was the head of gold of the great colossus that the king had seen in his dream. The Babylonian Empire came to an end when the conquering armies of the Medes and the Persians killed Nebuchadnezzar's grandson, Belshazzar. This happened the very evening he had seen the vision of a hand writing on the wall, the night the great city of Babylon fell. It has remained in ruins ever since.

However, many have predicted that Babylon will be reconstructed in these last days. When Saddam Hussein made the statement that he was a direct descendant of Nebuchadnezzar, he began trying to restore Babylon. Many students of the Bible began rejoicing when they heard the news and believed they were about to witness the fulfillment of another Biblical prophecy. If Babylon is to be destroyed in the last days, as predicted in Revelation, it means it would first of all have to be reconstructed. Today Saddam Hussein is much too busy, arming for another war with the United States or with Israel, to be taken up with the reconstruction of old Babylon. In Jeremiah 50 and 51 God revealed to the prophet in great detail the fate of the Babylon the Great. Talking about the destruction of the city God says in Jeremiah 50: 35 and 40, *"A sword is upon the Chaldeans, saith the LORD, and upon the inhabitants of Babylon, and upon her princes, and upon her wise men. As God overthrew Sodom and Gomorrah and the neighbour cities thereof, saith the LORD; so shall no man abide there, neither shall any son of man dwell therein."* Sodom and Gomorrah were never rebuilt nor ever again inhabited and thus shall it always be with ancient Babylon. In fact, in verse 39 of the same chapter God says that very thing, *"and it shall be **no more inhabited** for ever; neither shall it be dwelt in from generation to generation."*

If ancient Babylon can never be rebuilt nor inhabited, then the mention of Babylon in the book of Revelation must refer to some other city in existence today. When we read the description of this city in Revelation 17, God compares it to a prostitute. Verses 4–6 tell us: *"And the woman was arrayed in purple and scarlet colour, and decked with gold and precious stones and pearls, having a golden cup in her hand full of abominations and filthiness of her fornication: and upon her forehead was a name written, MYSTERY, BABYLON THE GREAT, THE MOTHER OF HARLOTS AND ABOMINATIONS OF THE EARTH. And I saw the woman drunken with the blood of the saints, and with the blood of the martyrs of Jesus."*

Babylon Is Rome

The woman, by all serious students of the Bible, has been identified as the Vatican in Rome. In that short description, we find several clues to help us in identifying the city in question. First of all, we note that the woman is arrayed in purple and scarlet–the two outstanding colors of The Roman Catholic Church. Then we read that she is decked with gold and precious pearls which speak of her great riches. Few realize the great wealth of the Vatican. She owns great quantities of stock in most of the leading companies of the world. Just recently the news media announced that the Vatican owns more property in New York City than any other organization or individual. The value of the golden chalices tucked away in churches all over Europe cannot even be estimated. In the Vatican library are documents and manuscripts that are priceless.

"...Having a golden cup in her hand full of abominations and filthiness of her fornication." (Revelation 17:4) This fornication is described as being with the *"kings of the earth"* (Verse 2). On the day of Pentecost, the Church was independent of the State. It had the power of the Holy Spirit upon it and announced freely the message of salvation to both Jew and Gentile. Thousands believed in Christ and were willing to follow Him in spite of the persecution of the Roman Empire. But when the Emperor Constantine entered Rome in the year 312, he decreed that all persecuton of Christians must stop and the following year, through the Edict of Milan, he gave to every man the freedom to follow the religion of his choice.

At first Christians hailed this as a tremendous victory, but soon discovered there was a worm in the apple. Emperor Constantine annexed Christianity to the State and thus began a marriage that led immediately to apostasy. Infant baptism was quickly adopted. Everyone was now a "Christian," even if he was never born again. True believers, who wanted to be in fellowship with others of like faith, soon found themselves persecuted once again–only this time it was not by the pagan Roman Empire, but by the pagan Roman Catholic Church.

We come now to the most outstanding of the clues when we read that she is *"...drunken with the blood of the saints and with the blood of the martyrs of Jesus..."* (Revelation 17:6) Nowhere in the world has this been proved more true than in France, where they persecuted the Vaudois, the Albigensions and the Beghards. In a very short time in French history, the Catholics tortured and put to death more than one million true believers in that one country alone! Under the direction of the high dignitaries of the Catholic Church and led militarily by Simon de Montfort, a very capable man but excessively cruel and ambitious, they ravaged the most beautiful and most cultured land in Europe during a 20-year period.

When the Protestants fled for refuge to the city of Bezier in Southern France, they were able to live in peace with the Catholics in that city. Simon de Montfort arrived at Bezier and was about to launch his attack when he found out that there were many Catholics residing peacefully there with the Protestants. He contacted the Catholic prelate over that area of France to know what to do under those circumstances. The answer was not long in coming: "Kill them all, God will recognize His own." And thus all the inhabitants of that city were slain.

The Catholic Church has had "fornication" with the heads of State throughout all of that church's history. Most of the time, the Church was completely *linked* with the *"kings of the earth."* The fact of the Church being married to the State, was so deeply rooted in the hearts and minds of everyone that even the Reformers, John Calvin, Zwingly and Martin Luther could not conceive of the Church and State being separated. They followed the Catholic teaching in this manner, trying to replace Catholic countries by creating Protestant ones to the extent that they, too, ended up by persecuting, and in some cases even to death, the Baptists and non-conconformist believers.

The harlot is also pictured as sitting *"upon a scarlet coloured beast, full of names of blasphemy, having seven heads and ten horns."* (Revelation 17:3) The Beast is described later as being the revived Roman Empire composed of ten nations. The World Religion will come into power by riding on the back of the World Government, which at that time will be under the control of the Antichrist. At this present time, the Pope is doing all he can to try to unite the great religions of the world by making pilgrimages to Athens to win the Orthodox Church and to Amman to try to win the Moslems. Even if Pope John Paul II dies before being able to accomplish his goal, his successor will carry on the project until all religions of the Western nations will be united and cooperating fully with the world government.

One event that is often overlooked when reading this 17th chapter of Revelation is the fact that the world political force of the ten united nations, headed up by the Antichrist, will destroy the Vatican. *"And the ten horns which thou sawest upon the beast, these shall hate the whore, and shall make her desolate and naked, and shall eat her flesh, and burn her with fire."* (Verse 16) The Antichrist will not tolerate sharing his power and glory with the Vatican, but will, out of jealousy, completely destroy the Catholic Church. Nebuchadnezzar demanded that he not only be obeyed, but ***worshipped.*** This was true with the Caesars of the Roman Empire. Paul presented Jesus Christ as God, the only One to be worshipped. He refused to bow down to the Emperor even as did Shadrach, Meshach, and Abednego refuse to bow down before the great statue of Nebuchadnezzar. Paul, because of this, was martyred. The Antichrist will destroy the Vatican because he will want everyone to worship him. He will refuse to share his glory with the Virgin Mary, the Saints, the Pope or with Jesus.

There Are Two Babylons in Revelation

Where does New York City come into all this? When we look carefully at Revelation 18 we find a totally different description from that found in chapter 17. The Babylon of chapter 17 is situated on seven hills for we read in verse 9, *"And here is the mind which hath wisdom. The seven heads are seven mountains, on which the woman sitteth."* Rome is known as the city that sits on seven hills. But when we study the 18th chapter we find a maritime city dealing in all kinds of merchandise. Rome isn't, nor ever has been, a maritime city. The passage in Revelation 18 talks about merchants doing business there, *"And the merchants of the earth shall weep and mourn over her; for no man buyeth their merchandise any more:"* (verse 11), then in verse 17 we read, *"For in one hour so great riches is come to nought. And every shipmaster, and all the company in ships, and sailors, and as many as trade by sea, stood afar off."*

The city is also described as being very rich (verse 12) and as being a port that can be seen from the sea. Notice verses 18 and 19, where the merchants when they see the city being judged by God cry out, *"And cried when they saw the smoke of her burning, saying, What city like unto this great city! And they cast dust on their heads, and cried, weeping and wailing, saying, Alas, alas, that great city, wherin were made rich all that had ships in the sea by reason of her costliness! for in one hour is she made desolate."* No other maritime city can compare to New York. Ships can come up the Hudson River to the center of Manhattan Island. Great ships like the *Queen Mary*, the *Queen Elizabeth*, the *Mauritania* and others would actually dock at the beginning of 42nd Street with the possibility of a relatively easy walk from there to Times Square!

New York is fabulously rich. New York is a maritime city made rich by its world commerce. New York is a port that can be seen from afar off. New York is the home of the United Nations, the center of world politics. New York is the home of the Wall Street money market that controls world commerce. It is said in Paris that when Wall Street coughs, Europe comes down with the flu. There are three great powers in the world: Politics, Commerce and Religion. This one great metropolis already houses two of the three. When the Antichrist destroys Rome, it is very probable that he will move the headquarters of his world religion to New York, so that all three of the great powers of the world will be concentrated in one place. Of one thing we are sure–the Babylon of chapter 17 is definitely not the one found in chapter 18. Besides the differences that have already been mentioned, we must also note that the Babylon of chapter 17 will be destroyed by the ten horns and the Beast, whereas the one in Chapter 18 will be destroyed by God Himself, *"Therefore shall her plagues come in one day, death, and mourning, and famine; and she shall be utterly burned with fire: for strong is the Lord God who judgeth her."* (Revelation 18:8)

What was just a thought that crossed my mind in 1946 as I stared at the skyline of *"The Great City"* eventually became a conviction. The problem that faces everyone interested in Biblical prophecy is, if New York is not Babylon the Great, then what other great maritime city in the world today could replace it–the criteria are demanding.

PART THREE - PARABLES IN MATTHEW

Hear another parable. (Matthew 21:33)

Another parable put he forth unto them.
(Matthew 13:24)

But without a parable spake he not unto them.
(Mark 4:34)

1

The Parables of Matthew

"Jesus was putting the cookies on the lower shelf when He gave the Parables," explained a pastor as he began his studies in Matthew 13. However, he couldn't have been further from the truth. The parables were never intended to be windows or illustrations to Christ's teaching, but rather His way of hiding His truth from those who would have loved to tread his pearls under foot. This is exactly what Christ was saying in Matthew 13:10–13 where we read, *"And the disciples came, and said unto him, Why speakest thou unto them in parables? He answered and said unto them, Because it is given unto you to know the mysteries of the kingdom of heaven, but to them it is not given...Therefore speak I to them in parables: because they seeing see not: and hearing they hear not, neither do they understand."*

Then again it is recorded in Matthew 13:34 *"All these things spake Jesus unto the multitude in parables; and without a parable spake he not unto them."* To the crowds that gathered around Him, Christ spoke in parables to hide His truth, but to His disciples He explained the parables or spoke in words they could easily understand as recorded in Mark 4:10–12 *"And when he was alone, they that were about him with the twelve asked of him the parable. And he said unto them, Unto you it is given to know the mystery of the kingdom of God: but unto them that are without, all these things are done in parables: That seeing they may see, and not perceive; and hearing they many hear, and not understand."*

Why include the parables in this book devoted to prophecy is a question that many might be asking at this point. The parables of our Lord, in mystery form, were to reveal what would happen to His teachings after His death, burial and ressurrection. We shall discover, as we go through the parables, that they cover the entire scope of the Church Age and reveal the effects that false doctrines will have on His teachings. These parables are definitely prophetic and throw more light on what we have already discovered.

Another reason we have been encouraged to cover this material, after visiting many churches in Europe and in the United States, is the apparent lack of a clear understanding of the parables. Many wonderful messages are preached from Matthew 13 drawing rich comparisons from life-situations today, linking them to one of the parables and thus edifying the believers. This is all to their credit, but giving illustrations drawn from the parables does not give their true meaning and thus most often leaves the people with a wrong conception of what Christ was really teaching. Before ever using a parable as an illustration, the true meaning must be given so as not to leave the audience in the dark as to its true interpretation. It is because of not giving the true interpretation before drawing illustrations that false doctrines are circulating today in churches all over the world. We know that very good commentaries have already been written on the subject, but it is evident that they have not been read by most church members, and without any doubt, even by many pastors. Many of these great commentaries are no longer in print and this is a subject that is not appealing to church members as much as books on "Christian psychology" and counsel for newlyweds and couples in trouble. In fact, today it is hard to find any good commentaries or Bible study material in the average Christian book store and this is true not only in the United States, but in Europe as well. All this is creating weak Christians who do not know how to defend the faith and will not be able to stand firm for Christ in a day of persecution.

The Kingdom of Heaven

The expression "the Kingdom of Heaven" is found throughout the Gospel of Matthew, whereas we find the words "The Kingdom of God" being used in Luke's Gospel when he recounts the same parable. The "Kingdom of Heaven" is a more restricted title than the one used by Luke. The "Kingdom of God" embraces God's sovereign rule over the universe from eternity to eternity and "The Kingdom of Heaven" was used for the ears of the Jewish people and is the fulfillment of Old Testament prophecy relating the coming of the Messiah and His Millennial reign. The "mystery" parables *reveal events that will lead up to Christ's thousand-year reign* which were not disclosed in the pages of the Old Testament.

There are those who teach that the only books in the Bible for the church today are the Epistles of Paul. For them, one can just tear out the other pages of the Holy Writ for they have nothing to do with us. On the other hand, we have millions of others who take every word in the Old Testament, as well as in the New, to be directly applied to themselves. (Hear me now: Every chapter and every line in the whole Bible was *"written for our instruction"* and can be a great blessing for us as well as illustrations of what to do and or not do. The Bible is filled with promises we can take for ourselves and watch God work, but every verse is not to be applied directly to us who are living in the Age of Grace.) This is what "dividing the Word of Truth" is all about. This is what dispensational teaching is all about. We benefit from all the Bible without coming under every judgment pronounced and every law given.

The Kingdom of Heaven Is Not the Church

This having been said, we must remember, as we read the parables in Matthew, that wherever the expression, "The Kingdom of Heaven" is used, we are not to replace those words by taking that expression to mean the "Church that was formed at Pentecost." Yes, we can draw many illustrations for our daily living from those wonderful words of our Lord, without trying to fit them in, as one tries to force a piece into the picture of a jigsaw puzzle that was definitely not cut for that spot. This is exactly where so many of our false doctrines find their origin. Wrong interpretation of Matthew, the Acts of the Apostles, Hebrews and the Corinthian letters have become the source of almost all false doctrines circulating among Christians throughout the world today.

We will now begin our study of the "mystery" parables in Matthew 13.

2

The Sower

And he spake many things unto them in parables, saying,
Behold, a sower went forth to sow; And when he sowed,
some seeds fell by the way side, and the fowls came and
devoured them up: Some fell upon stony places,...and
forthwith they sprung up, because they had no deepness of
earth: And when the sun was up, they were scorched; and
because they had no root, they withered away. And some
fell among thorns; and the thorns sprung up, and choked
them: But other fell into good ground, and brought forth
fruit, some an hundredfold, some sixtyfold, some
thirtyfold. Who hath ears to hear, let him hear.
Matthew 13:3–9

This first parable in chapter 13 is not a prophetic one as are the
others that follow, but it definitely lays the foundation. Of all the
parables in this chapter, this is the easiest of them to explain, especially since our Lord spelled it out very clearly to His disciples in
verses 18 through 23. What must be clearly understood from the
beginning is that the Sower is our Lord. Secondly, we must understand that the seed is the Word of God, but the emphasis must be
placed on the fact that it is His doctrine or teaching that is being sown.

We must always keep in mind that Christ's message was the
Gospel of the Kingdom of Heaven and not the Gospel of the Grace
of God we preach today. Today we preach Christ crucified for our

sins and risen for our justification. Christ could not have preached that message because He still hadn't died on the cross nor was He risen from the dead. His message to the Jews of His time was the same as that of John the Baptist, *"Repent: for the Kingdom of Heaven is at hand."* (Matthew 4:17)

The Results Depend on the Soil, not on the Seed

The results of the sowing depended not on the value of the seed, but on the ground upon which it fell. The same seed fell on different soils and therefore the results were different.

That same truth applies today as it did when Christ was sowing. We can go out sowing the same Gospel message wherever we go and yet find different results. People react differently to the same presentation of the Word of God, depending on where in the world it is being preached. In Eastern Europe it is much more readily received than in Western Europe. In South American countries as well as in many countries in Africa, the Word is readily received, whereas in Moslem countries it is almost impossible to bring souls to Christ. Even in the same country, evangelists and pastors can pour out their hearts before an audience and while some come forward weeping at the invitation, others remain cold and indifferent, but it doesn't stop there. Even later, when considering the final results, they are often much different from what they seemed to be during the special meetings. Many who appeared to have opened their hearts to Christ are never seen any more in the services. Something happened in the meantime. This is what this parable teaches and has taught down through the centuries.

The Seed by the Way Side

There are still people like those "who receive the seed by the way side." Satan is always quick to catch away the precious seed. These are people who are momentarily drawn to the simplicity and urgency of the message, but once outside the building all is forgotten. There are so many things that flood their minds and demand their immediate attention. Especially is this true of those who listened to the message for the first time but weren't able to grasp the full impact of what they had just heard. In France, where the true Gospel is virtually unknown, we find those who tell us after the service how much they enjoyed it, but seldom do they ever return. Satan quickly caught away the seed. They just "received the seed by the way side."

The Seed in Stony Places

Then there are those who receive the seed "into stony places." The Lord says that they joyfully receive the Word but since they have no root in themselves, even though they continue for a while, when tribulation or persecution arises they are offended and drop off. We who work in France find it very difficult to win a soul to Christ, but it is even harder to get that person grounded in the Word and coming faithfully to Church. They seem to have no roots in themselves. Just the smallest obstacle, that seems to momentarily block their path, is all it takes to stop their attendance at church. Their "tribulations and persecutions" can often be boiled down to someone neglecting to greet them when they enter the church building, or by something the pastor might have said which they took as being directed at them.

Real tribulations and persecutions in a country make people think before they come to Christ for salvation. But once the decision is made, they seem to be strengthened when they face persecution. They become stalwart Christians totally engaged in their churches and in the advancement of the Kingdom of God. Many pastors have been overheard to say they actually wished there were some sort of persecution in the United States and Europe. This would make Christians take a real stand for Christ as they must do in China, Nepal, Saudi Arabia and all other countries living under Islam, Hinduism and Communism where people are being tortured for their faith and suffering martyrdom.

There is much propaganda, especially since China has been chosen for the 2008 Olympics, saying that there is more freedom of religion there now than previously. However, the director of one of the leading missions working in the Orient, recently told us that the situation is getting worse. National pastors are being imprisoned and tortured and 6,000 places of worship were destroyed in the year 2000! Prayer is the greatest weapon on earth. All Christians who know how to pray should be intereceding daily for our fellow believers in those countries where they are suffering for their faith.

The Seed Among the Thorns

"He also that received seed among the thorns is he that heareth the word; and the care of this world, and the deceitfulness of riches, choke the word, and he becometh unfruitful." (verse 22) This phrase coming from the lips of our Lord describes explicitly what happened to a wonderful young couple in one of our churches in France. They came faithfully to church every Sunday, with their four young daughters, and he became one of the deacons. Then, for no apparent reason, the whole family stopped coming. Phone calls and visits were always graciously received, but with no results. What happened? *"The deceitfulness of riches"* had taken hold on this whole family and extinguished their light.

Materialism is the main sickness gripping the Church in the free countries today. It is like gangrene or cancer wearing down the effectiveness of Christians. It has a numbing effect that is hard to detect. Christians are not realizing that their presence before the unsaved is bearing little fruit. Young people are becoming numb to the call to foreign missions. They reason that life today offers too much, to give their life in some far off country. People are going to church by the millions in the United States, but all this has very little effect in stopping the decline of morals or the apostacy that is sweeping the land. In Europe, many who once stood firm for Christ have now left the church in search of something "more exciting."

When the Lord led us to begin a Baptist Church in Toulouse, France, which is close to the Spanish border, we witnessed first-hand the effect that materialism can have on consecrated Christians. Just a few years before we arrived in that city, General Francisco Franco had come to power and the Christians in Spain were being persecuted. All this had a cleansing effect on the believers and they became bold in their faith and desirous to make Christ known to everyone. Many fled to France at that time and some located in Toulouse. Some of these Christians found our church and asked permission to hold meetings there in Spanish. They were "on fire" for the Lord and soon learned the French language and became part of our French assembly. As these Christians tasted more freedom in France, they quickly became accustomed to the materialism that existed there. They eventually lost their fire and their "first love" and settled down to average Christian living that we all know so well.

How true it is that Christians who can live for Christ under persecution, fall under the temptation of materialism. Paul said, *"I know both how to be abased, and I know how to abound: every where and in all things I am instructed both to be full and to be hungry, both to abound and to suffer need."* (Philippians 4:12) In the early years of my ministry, I could see how easy it was for Paul to live in abundance, but how hard it must have been for him to live for Christ in poverty. How greatly my opinion has changed. Christians suffering for Christ in difficult lands are abounding in the Grace of our Lord, whereas the multitude of those who call themselves Christians in America and in other wealthy nations have lost their flame. The Lord is saying to His church today, as He said in the days of the Apostle John, *"Repent, and do the first works; or else I will come unto thee quickly, and will remove thy candlestick out of his place, except thou repent."* (Revelation 2:5)

The Seed in Good Soil

Praise God, the parable does not end there. We read that there was seed that fell on good ground and those that heard and understood went forth to bear fruit—some thirty percent, some sixty and finally there were those who produced an hundredfold. The Lord encourages His people by saying, *"...be ye steadfast, unmoveable, always abounding in the work of the Lord, forasmuch as **ye know that your labour is not in vain in the Lord.**"* (1 Corinthians 15:58). What a wonderful promise for those who labor in difficult places. Our mind goes to those who spent a lifetime winning but one or two souls to Christ as was the case in past years for those who labored in countries dominated by Islam. We know there are more results today because of radio and also the fact that many from those countries have visited other lands where the Word of God is preached freely, but it is still soil that yields little fruit.

However, the same results occur when the seed is sown in the same country, in the same town and in the same church. Why do some Christians produce more fruit than others? Perhaps it would be proper at this time to define what is meant here by the word "fruit." In Galatians 5:22 we read, *"But the fruit of the Spirit is love, joy, peace, longsuffering, gentleness, goodness, faith..."* Is this the fruit Christ is talking about in this parable? It is true that all who name the Name of Christ should bear the fruit of the Spirit and live sanctified lives separated from the world, but this is not the explanation the Lord intends us to understand in this parable.

The Lord is asking His children to go out and witness to what He has done in their lives. We are to work in cooperation with the Holy Spirit to bring souls to Christ. *"The fruit of the righteous is a tree of life; and **he that winneth souls** is wise."* (Proverbs 11:30) The last words of our Lord recorded in Matthew 28:19 are *"Go ye therefore, and teach all nations, baptizing them in the name of the Father, and of the Son, and of the Holy Ghost."* We learn here that our mission is not even completed when we have won precious souls, but we are also to disciple and baptize them into a local church where they can continue to grow in the knowledge of the Word. Too many churches and organizations today are forgetting the second part of the Great Commission. First of all, we are not seeing many true conversions anymore. People are making "decisions for Christ," but the Holy Spirit had not as yet preprared their hearts by convicting them of sin, righteousness and judgment. They were asked to pray, but they don't really understand what they are praying for. With the result that millions today believe they are saved because they prayed and were baptized, but were never really born again. Then, added to that, many who do repent and accept Christ into their lives have never been discipled and do not know how to lead other souls to Christ. Many produce no fruit, some do produce thirty percent, but very, very few ever see an hundredfold.

3

The Tares

Another parable put he forth unto them, saying, The
kingdom of heaven is likened unto a man which sowed
good seed in his field: But while men slept, his enemy came
and sowed tares among the wheat, and went his way. But
when the blade was sprung up, and brought forth fruit,
then appeared the tares also. So the servants of the
householder came and said unto him, Sir, didst not thou
sow good seed in thy field? from whence then hath it tares?
He said unto them, An enemy hath done this. The servants
said unto him, Wilt thou then that we go and gather them
up? But he said, Nay; lest while ye gather up the tares, ye
root up also the wheat with them. Let both grow together
until the harvest: and in the time of harvest I will say to the
reapers, Gather ye together first the tares, and bind them
in bundles to burn them: but gather the wheat into my
barn. Matthew 13:24–30

We have come to the first of the prophetic parables. The Lord
will now reveal what is to become of the good seed that was sown.
At first sight, the parable of the Sower and that of the Tares resemble each other. We see again a sower going forth to plant his
seed and we discover that the Sower in both of them is the Lord.
(verse 37) We also see that the field is the world. (verse 38) Then

He gives a clear explanation of these first two parables. But the differences are even greater. First of all, the *seed* is different. In the first parable, the *seed* was Christ's Message—the Word of God presented as the Gospel of the Kingdom. Whereas in the second parable, we learn through Christ's explanation (verses 36-43), that the seed are *"the children of the kingdom."*

The Seed Becomes Christ's Disciples

The *seed* is now embodied in the lives of men and women who will go forth into the world to proclaim His message. Secondly, there is another sower, the Devil who will also be active. His seed will be in the form of tares and weeds that will try to choke out the future crop. Thirdly, we see the servants of the Lord asking if they should rip out those tares before they do any more damage, but the Lord says that they should leave them alone for the time being. Lastly, this parable takes us to the end of this Age of Grace where we see the outcome of this wicked deed of the enemy. The angels will gather together first the tares and bind them in bundles to burn, but then they will gather the wheat into His *barn*. (But what a barn!) The description of this *barn* is given us in Revelation 21 where we read in verse 2, *"And I John saw the holy city, new Jerusalem, coming down from God out of heaven, prepared as a bride adorned for her husband."* Our Lord has been preparing a *place* for His bride for the last 2000 years and He will soon be taking her Home.

Errors in the Early Church

The enemy sowed these tares or false doctrines immediately after the good seed was sown. The major object, in virtually all the Epistles of the New Testament, was to correct some false teaching that was already circulating in the first century. Jude was particularly aware of this danger. We read in veres 3 and 4, *"Beloved, when I gave all diligence to write unto you of the common salvation, it was needful for me to write unto you, and exhort you that ye should earnestly* **contend for the faith** *which was once delivered unto the saints. For there are certain men crept in unawares, who were before of old ordained to this condemnation, ungodly men, turning the grace of our God into las-*

civiousness, and denying the only Lord God, and our Lord Jesus Christ." The apostle Paul said in 2 Timothy 1:13 *"Hold fast the form of sound words, which thou hast heard of me, in faith and love which is in Christ Jesus."*

Paul had to continually defend the faith. In the book of Galatians he had to stand against those who were saying that men are saved by Grace, but are kept and sanctified by the Law. This is why we read in chapter 3:1-3 *"O foolish Galatians, who hath bewitched you, that ye should not obey the truth, before whose eyes Jesus Christ hath been evidently set forth, crucified among you? This only would I learn of you, Received ye the Spirit by the works of the law, or by the hearing of faith? Are ye so foolish?* **having begun in the Spirit, are ye now made perfect by the flesh?**" It is in this same book that he mentions having to reprove the Apostle Peter because he was compromising his position in Christ and acting the hypocrite by refusing to eat with the Gentiles when the Jews from Jerusalem were present. Here again he was fighting Judaism being mixed with the Message of Grace.

Division in the Church

Throughout the whole book of 1 Corinthians he had to correct one error after another which was springing up in that assembly like tares among the wheat. The first attack of Satan came in the form of division among the brethren because different groups were forming in the church, each contending to be more spiritual than the other. Haven't we all seen this very thing happen in churches we have known? Probably the best weapon Satan has against the local church is division.

A united, praying church, is awesome, *"terrible as an army with banners"* (Song of Solomon 6:4) and able to destroy the fortresses of Satan. Great revivals throughout all of church history have been the fruit of God's children being united and praying earnestly in faith. However, a divided church is as feeble as a crippled fawn trying to flee from the hunter. Every church should strive for unity and purity because God will then bless His children. *"No good thing will He withhold from them that walk uprightly."* (Psalm 84:11) Miracles are still possible. Christians deprive themselves of seeing God work mightily in their midst simply because they have so little faith in the God of the impossible and do not strive for unity.

The Danger of Human Wisdom

From there Paul goes on in the second and third chapters to reveal a fact that most Christians today have totally forgotten. Human wisdom was lifting its head against the revealed Word of God and trying to replace it. Powerful preaching is not the result of human wisdom nor education, but the fruit of Spirit-filled messages given by a man of God. Paul had just learned that lesson when he wrote this Epistle. He had been in Athens on Mars Hill where he gave a great oration. (Acts 17) There, before the philosophers, the Epicureans and the Stoics of that city, he spoke of the God who created the heavens and the earth, he taught them that they should not worship idols made by man, he cited one of their poets, he spoke of the UNKNOWN GOD who had raised a Man from the dead and before whom every human being will have to stand in judgment. The results of that message were small. There is no record in the New Testament of any church ever being established in that city. However, Paul had learned his lesson.

When he went to Corinth, his message changed completely. Notice what he says to them in 1 Corinthians 2:1–5, *"And I, brethren, when I came to you, came not with excellency of speech or of wisdom, declaring unto you the testimony of God.* (He could have there inserted, "As I did in Athens") ***For I determined not to know any thing among you, save Jesus Christ, and him crucified.*** *And I was with you in weakness, and in fear, and in much trembling. And my speech and my preaching was not with enticing words of man's wisdom, but in demonstration of the Spirit and of power:* ***That your faith should not stand in the wisdom of men, but in the power of God."*** How many preachers, standing behind pulpits today, would do well to just put aside their personal elequence and the evident display of their great education, and just preach Christ and Christ crucified. Many more souls would be saved and saints edified.

Education, like money, is not evil in itself, but if it's not totally given over to the Lord, it can destroy a man's ministry. If one leans on what he learned in the higher schools of education, rather than on the Lord for inspiration and power, the results will be the same as those of Paul on Mars Hill. There is definitely too much emphasis on education today rather than on the power of the Holy Spirit and the results are being reaped the world over. We see many "decisions" for Christ, but few genuine conversions. Strong believers are not built up in their faith by well-worded sermons, but by messages that come straight from heaven. Holy Spirit-filled pastors and evangelists are hard to find these days.

Yes, Paul had studied at the feet of Gamaliel, and we should not forbid higher education; however, we cannot help but recognize that the spiritual level of Christians today is far below where it was a hundred years ago. Christians, on the whole, are not witnessing to their friends and neighbors. We are no longer seeing great revivals that not only sweep thousands into the Kingdom of God, but also transform whole cities and communities. They are forgetting the millions in far-off mission fields without God and without hope, who will die in their sins and be lost forever unless believers stop living self-centered lives and young people begin once again begin consecrating themselves to go wherever Christ would send them.

The Scarlet Sin

Many were the iniquities and weaknesses of this Corinthian church and among them we find the sin of fornication, and as Paul says in verse 1 of chapter 5, *"It is reported commonly that there is fornication among you, and such fornication as is not so much as named among the Gentiles, that one should have his father's wife."* Yes, here we are with the "scarlet sin." This sin is so common today, even among believers, that Christians are not even shocked when someone falls into it. This sin is pictured on TV as being the normal thing. In France they say, "Who isn't unfaithful to his wife today? Or what young person hasn't been into this sin before marriage?" It won't be long before they will be saying this in America as well. Some claim that it is already being said.

Another sexual sin that is considered by God to be much worse than adultery or fornication is that of sodomy, called homosexuality today or just "gay." This is what Paul says about this sin in

Romans 1:18, 25–27, *"For the wrath of God is revealed from heaven against all ungodliness and unrighteousness of men, who hold the truth in unrighteousness; Who changed the truth of God into a lie, and worshipped and served the creature more than the Creator, who is blessed for ever, Amen. For this cause God gave them up unto vile affections: for even their women did change the natural use into that which is against nature: And likewise also the men, leaving the natural use of the woman, burned in their lust one toward another: men with men working that which is unseemly, and receiving in themselves that recompence of their error* (AIDS, which homosexuals refuse to admit) *which was meet."*

In France, it is now against the law to speak out against this blight without running the risk of being fined or even receiving a jail sentence. Every Bible-believing pastor must have the courage to speak out against this "sin" (and remember this is not a sickness, as some like to consider it). It is a sin that will be severely judged by God. With multitudes marching openly down the streets in Paris, in San Francisco, and yes, even in Charlotte, NC in the heart of the "Bible Belt," it is getting harder and harder to sing, "God Bless America." Why should He keep heaping blessings on this nation that is forgetting God and His Word?

If it were not for the United States standing up before the other nations in defense of Israel, and if it were not for their support given to thousands of missionaries around the world, God's Hand of judgment would already have struck this nation! America, along with France and other European countries, must brace herself for the wrath of God that will soon be poured out against all this ungodliness and outright flaunting of His Word. Why are we mentioning this sin as a tare in the church today? Because there are now churches that are condoning it and even homosexual pastors in pulpits both in Europe and in the United States!

Sexual Sins are Not the Only Sins

Pastors and evangelists must be careful not to consider sexual sin to be the *only* sin. Whether it be in France or in the United States, if one is accused of sin, it usually means some sexual sin. This is a danger all Christians must beware of. It is becoming more and more a fact, that if one keeps himself from that one sin, he can virtually commit all others. A pastor is never asked to leave his pulpit because of sin, unless it is sexual. He is not asked to leave because he is proud, or because he is self-seeking, jealous, personally ambitious, loves money or runs the church like a dictator. However, these sins, just mentioned, usually finish by destroying a church. More assemblies are ruined by the "tongue" than by some member committing sexual sin. If you check around you will find that divisions usually come through pride, jealousy and self-seeking.

We must never condone the "scarlet sin." It must be judged and the guilty person must repent and ask forgiveness, **but then the church must be ready to forgive him.** (This is exactly what Paul was saying to the church in Corinth about what to do with this man who had committed that terrible sin.) We read in 2 Corinthians 2:6–11: *"Sufficient to such a man is this punishment, which was inflicted of many. So that contrariwise ye ought rather **to forgive him**, and **comfort him**, lest perhaps such a one should be swallowed up with overmuch sorrow. Wherefore I beseech you that ye would confirm your love toward him. For to this end also did I write, that I might know the proof of you, whether ye be obedient in all things. To whom ye forgive any thing, I forgive also: for if I forgave any thing, to whom I forgave it, for your sakes forgave I it in the person of Christ; Lest Satan should get an advantage of us: for we are not ignorant of his devices."*

Churches today are having a very hard time forgiving a person who commits that sin. Sometimes they are "forgiven," but henceforth treated as "second class" members. We must remember two things: this particular transgression is not the unpardonable sin as many consider it today, for the blood of Christ washes away that sin, as well as all the others; secondly, there are other horrible iniquities that remain unjudged. Satan fell because of pride and was cast out of God's presence because of pride, not because of some sexual sin. Pride, with its many heads, is the principal sin that is destroying the church today.

Every Man of God who preaches the Word must be clothed with humility. Peter in his first Epistle in chapter 5, verse 6 says: *"Humble yourselves therefore under the mighty hand of God, that he may exalt you in due time."* This is not a suggestion, but a commandment, but oh, how hard it is to put it into practice. In the world, humilty is considered a weakness and men must display their importance. This is especially true in France, where men feel they are above any need of God in their lives–they have everything under control. The spirit of the world seems to have a way of rubbing off on God's children. Peter says we are to let God exalt us and not to elevate ourselves.

This spirit of pride is revealed in the lives of God's servants when we witness that very few are ever willing to take second place. For them, it's first place or nothing. It is much harder to find someone to play second violin than it is to find someone ready to play first. It is told that Caesar, when riding down the muddy little streets of Lutecia (the ancient name for Paris), turned to one of the officers in his army and said, "See this ugly village, I would rather be 'number one' here than number two in Rome." How much this spirit has taken hold of us today. I respect and honor men of value who could be pastors in their own rights, but who accept to be assistant pastors so that a greater work for God may be built. It is because of consecrated, humble men, ready to play "second fiddle," that most all renowned churches have become known throughout the world. These servants of God are very seldom praised, or even known, but without them God's great blessing would never have fallen on that special work. May God grant His Church more humble workers.

Other Tares in the Church

Paul also had to deal with other problems in that Corinthian church such as meat that had been offered to idols and was being sold in the market places, the different problems surrounding marriage, the disorder that reigned at the time of the communion service as well as whether those in his team should be allowed to bring their wives with them when they traveled from city to city. But we will limit ourselves with the last two big problems in this letter, since they are so prophetic, reaching into our churches today and wrecking havoc with many. We are talking about the "tongues movement" and the blessed truth of the resurrection.

The Tongues Movement

The Charismatic movement has divided the true church in the last century more than any other factor. It has grown from just a small beginning about 50 years ago to where it now includes most evangelical churches around the world. Millions are speaking in tongues these days who know nothing of the saving grace of our Lord! Roman Catholics, who have never come to Calvary for salvation, have, by the tens of thousands in France, enthusiastically embraced this false doctrine and tell us now how their fervor in worshipping Mary has grown! None of them would ever think of leaving the Catholic Church to join a true Bible-believing assembly because as they say, "We are members of the only 'True Church' and the Pope is God's Vicar on this earth." If Roman Catholics are our "brothers and sisters in Christ," as many Evangelicals are claiming today, then my wife and I have wasted 53 years of our lives trying to bring them the Gospel in France. Several hundreds of them have been saved in our meetings, baptized, and are now living separated lives for Christ. They never cease to thank God for opening their eyes to a religion that would have taken them into a Christless eternity.

Here in his epistle, written nearly 2000 years ago, the Apostle Paul attacks this false doctrine that was already circulating in the Corinthian Church and by so doing stopped this teaching until it flamed up again in the 20th century. We will not go into a long explanation of this error because many books revealing its dangers have already been written. We will only mention that Paul refers to the speaking in tongues as "childish things" that are to be put away when one is an adult in Christ. Three chapters later he admonishes those Christians in Corinth, *"Watch ye, stand fast in the faith, **quit you like men**,* (act the man and stop being children), *be strong."* (1 Corinthians 16:13) When he ends chapter 13 he doesn't say, "And now abideth prophesies, tongues and knowledge"–these three subjects hadn't even been mentioned in those chapters. That is because they were to end with the childhood of the infant church and be replaced by other things in the adulthood of the church, that was to continue till the Lord returns to take her Home. The three things he was talking about throughout the entire chapter, as well as in the 12th and 14th chapters, *"And now abideth faith, hope, charity, these three; but the greatest of these is charity.*

The Resurection, the Capstone of Christianity

In the great 15th chapter, Paul makes it very clear that there will be a resurrection when the bodies of all believers will be transformed into Christ's image. Already there were those who were questioning it. Christ's resurrection, as well as that of the church, is still under attack, but praise God, after 2000 years, both of these truths remain and comprise the very foundation of Christianity today. In most Oriental countries, and now taught throughout Europe, is the doctrine of reincarnation. What a contrast in life is evident when observing the countries where the resurrection has been preached and where reincarnation is taught! In the Orient, people live in dire poverty, in complete darkness, and with faces reflecting the terrible sadness that reigns in their hearts; whereas in countries that have known true Christianity, we find a much higher standard of living and a spirit of joy. The death, burial and ressurrection of our Lord was the message of the disciples that brought down the Roman Empire and *"turned the whole world upside down"* in those first days of Christianity.

Satan did not limit his sowing of tares to the early church, but continued throughout the centuries that followed. The church was attacked by worldliness to the extent that in the year 156, Montanus, and others with him, began to protest. There was also the false teaching that Christ never had a real body, but was only spiritual. Even to this day there are new false doctrines trying to find their way into the church almost daily. New sects and cults are coming into being all the time and this will do so until the end of this age. **Christendom** is the name by which this mixture of the tares and wheat is known today.

4

The Grain of Mustard Seed

Another parable put He forth unto them, saying, The
kingdom of heaven is like to a grain of mustard seed, which
a man took, and sowed in his field: Which indeed is the
least of all seeds: but when it is grown, it is the greatest
among herbs, and becometh a tree, so that the birds of the
air come and lodge in the branches thereof.
Matthew 13:31–32

Our Lord explained the first two "mystery" parables, but
here we find no explanation. From now on, we are to use what
we already have learned from the first explanations to understand the following parables.

We know that the "man" in this parable still means our Lord.
He is the one who planted this grain of mustard seed. The mustard
seed is very small. Our Lord said on another occasion *"If ye have
faith as a grain of mustard seed, ye shall say unto this mountain, Remove
hence to yonder place; and it shall remove; and nothing shall be impossible
unto you."* (Matthew 17:20) In other words, "If your faith is no
bigger than a mustard seed, it is all it would take to move a mountain." A mustard seed resembles a very small part of a dry fallen
leaf. In fact, the two crumble up in the same way so that it would
be hard to distinguish which is which. However, the difference is
manifested when the two are planted. The small part of the dry
leaf just rots in the ground, whereas the mustard seed dies and a

plant comes up. Why is that? Because there is *life* in the mustard seed and the plant that comes forth is a beautiful picture of the resurrection. Real faith is alive and productive.

Christ planted a small seed—His small group of disciples. But soon there were many more added. This is the normal growth witnessed in the first two parables, but here we have something abnormal. Yes, a mustard plant comes up, but it is grotesque. A mustard plant is just a plant, not a tree! However, here we read, "*and waxed a great tree.*" (Luke 13:19) It has grown way out of proportion. It has become a monstrosity. What is the Lord telling us here? He is revealing that the message He was sowing in the world would quickly produce a Christendom that wouldn't represent true Christianity at all. He was predicting the marriage of the Church with the State that took place when the Emperor Constantine united the two. The word "Christ" is stamped upon this grotesque organization, but this union was not the work of the Holy Spirit. Though we can greatly rejoice when God moves in a miraculous way in the hearts of men and women producing unusual results in a short period of time, we can only observe that this new "mustard tree" which became the "Holy Roman Catholic Church" was not the fruit of the Holy Spirit, but rather the result of ambitious men.

The Roman Church was quick to "hide the light under a bushel." For more than a thousand years people were deprived of the Word of God. Those who were able to discover the True Light were immediately persecuted and put to death by the church which claimed its origin in Christ. Was it not He who planted the mustard seed? We will not give a thorough history of what happened during those dark ages because others, more informed than we, have related that terrible period by giving the very names of many who stood for the faith at the risk of their lives. They relate how true believers were forced to hold clandestine meetings in the forest and in caves. These great martyrs kept the light burning by going from home to home with this glorious message, defying the orders of the king or the bishop of the Roman Church.

The parable also adds that birds came and lodged in the branches of this tree. Birds, just mentioned alone like that, are to be understood as a negative omen. All students of the Word interpret these birds to mean false doctrines that came and found lodging in this New Church. Little by little, new doctrines and dogmas were added. We will now give the year that the different practices and dogmas were added to the Catholic Church.

300 - Prayers for the Dead

300 - Making the Sign of the Cross

375 - Worship of Saints and Angels

394 - Mass Instituted

431 - Marian Worship

500 - Priest Began Dressing Differently than Lay People.

526 - Extreme Unction

593 - Purgatory Doctrine Adopted

600 - Worship Conducted in Latin

600 - Prayers Directed to Mary

607 - Boniface III Made First Pope

709 - Kissing the Pope's Foot

786 - Worship of Idols and Relics

850 - The Use of Holy Water Began

995 - Canonization of Saints

998 - Fasting on Fridays and Lent

1079 - Celibacy of Priesthood

1090 - Prayer Beads

1184 - The Inquisition

1190 - Sale of Indulgences

1215 - Transubstantiation

1220 - Adoration of the Wafer as Host

1229 - Bible Forbidden to Lay People

1414 - Cup Forbidden to People at Communion

1439 - Purgatory Doctrine Now Decreed

1439 - Doctrine of Seven Sacraments Affirmed

1508 - Ave Maria Approved

1534 - Jesuit Order Founded

1545 - Tradition Granted Equal Authority with the Bible

1546 - Apocryphal Books Added to the Bible

1854 - Immaculate Conception
            (Mary's Mother Declared Sinless)

1864 - Syllabus of Errors Proclaimed

1870 - Infallibility of Pope Declared

1950 - Assumption of Mary (she never died)

1965 - Mary Proclaimed Mother of the Church

October 8, 2000 - Millennium Dedicated to Mary's care

It took the Catholic Church 1,950 years to discover that Mary was translated directly into heaven without dying! One day while walking through the Jewish quarter of Paris, le Marais, I thought I would go into a travel agency there to see if they had better fares to Israel than could be found elsewhere. While waiting to be served, I noticed a large brochure showing the most interesting places to visit while in Israel. One of them was Mary's tomb! Someone had forgotten to inform that agency that Mary had been taken up to heaven without dying and therefore never had a tomb! Until the time Mary's assumption was proclaimed in 1950, all good Catholics visited her tomb. The most respected of all French holidays is Assumption, the day they celebrate Mary's ascension into heven

All these additions to the doctrines found in the New Testament have made the Catholic Church into a false religion. One of their prelates declared years ago that the "The Catholic Church is a sect that has succeeded." Certainly it departed from the foundation that was laid by our Lord and His Apostles. It is not the intention of this book to expose all the false doctrines and practices of Catholicism, but we do feel that certain facts should be brought out at this time in order to more clearly illustrate what the unusual growth of the mustard seed produced.

In James G. McCarthy's very informative book on the dangers of Catholicism, *The Gospel According to Rome*[2] he points out how Rome changed completely the clear message of salvation, presented in the New Testament, to a system of works to obtain

---

[2] James G. McCarthy, *The Gospel According to Rome.* Harvest House Publishers, page 264.

merit in the eyes of he Lord. The Roman Church, adding one false teaching after another, like birds flying to a tree to find rest, finished by having two different foundations, the Word of God and Tradition. Little by little, tradition took precedence over the Word of God.

The Catholic Church reasons that since the Scriptures have always been progressive and were written by men inspired by the Spirit, why did that progressive inspiration end in the first century? They teach that the Magisterium has the power to make decisions concerning what is to be taught as doctrine and accepted by all Catholics. Here is a quotation in his book that recounts what happened in one of their Council meetings:

> As the last bishop took his seat, Gasser carefully reviewed his two main arguments. The first was that Christ gave Peter the ability to teach without error. This, he would argue, occurred when the Lord made Peter the head of the Apostles and of the universal church. The second point logically followed: since the Pope is Peter's successor, he is also heir to Peter's gift of infallibility.
>
> The ringing of the bell brought Bishop Gasser's preparation to a close. The First Vatican Council was in session.
>
> Bishop Gasser spoke elequently and with conviction that day, his speech taking four hours. When he finished he took his seat, fully aware of the historic significance of the moment.
>
> Bitter controversy followed. The Bishops rejected the first draft of the decree in a private vote; 88 bishops stood opposed. The document was sent back to the committee for revision.
>
> Five days later, after further debate, the bishops held another vote. This time they approved the decree: 533 in favor, 2 opposed. Henceforth, the Roman Catholic Church would teach that God had revealed that the Roman Pontiff is immune of even the possibility of teaching error. The decision would be irreversible, irreformable, and binding

upon Catholics everywhere. *Roma locuta est; causa finita est*–Rome has spoken; the case is closed."

By a simple vote, a new decree, binding on all Catholics is established. These decrees form the "second foundation" for their beliefs and this "second foundation" is called "tradition" by the Catholic Church.

In France, one day I asked a Roman Catholic priest, "Since the church has two different foundations for faith, if one were to contradict the other, to which one of the two would he refer?" He didn't hesitate a minute before replying, "I would choose our tradition."

For all who truly want to know what the Catholic Church teaches, we would also suggest a book written by Dave Hunt intitled, *A Woman Rides the Beast.*[3] He brings out very clearly the important role that Mary plays in that church. We quote now from this book:

> The most authoritative book written on Catholicism's Virgin Mary is by Cardinal and Saint Alphonsus de Liguori, titled *The Glories of Mary.* It is a virtual compendium of what the great "saints" of the Roman Catholic Church have had to say about Mary down through the centuries. The chapter headings are staggering, crediting Mary with attributes, abilities, titles, and functions that belong to Christ alone: "Mary, Our Life, Our Sweetness;" "Mary, Our Hope;" "Mary Our Help;" Mary, Our Advocate;" Mary, Our Guardian;" "Mary Our Salvation." Here is a sampling of Liguori's quotes of what the saints have said concerning Mary's role in salvation:
>
> "Sinners receive pardon by...Mary alone. He falls and is lost who has not recourse to Mary. Mary is called...the gate of heaven because no one can enter that blessed kingdom without passing through her. The way of salvation is open to none other than through Mary...the salvation of all depends on their being favored and protected by Mary. He who is protected by Mary will be saved; he who is

---

[3] Dave Hunt, *A Woman Rides the Beast.* Harvest House Publishers, pages 437–438.

not will be lost...our salvation depends on thee...God will not save us without the intercession of Mary... who would receive any grace were it not for thee, O Mother of God...?"

A Visit to Lourdes

It is deplorable and sad to realize how far the Roman Church has departed from the *"faith which was once delivered unto the saints."* (Jude 3) On several occasions we have visited the pilgrimage city of Lourdes, located in the Pyrenees mountains in southern France. Here is where the Virgin Mary is supposed to have appeared and where she is clearly worshipped by the millions who visit the site. There is the grotto (a cave) where Bernadette Soubirou, as a young girl, is suppose to have seen her and where many miracles since then are supposed to have taken place. We have witnessed people seeking healing at that spot and noticed the hundreds of crutches, blackened by the smoke from the numerous huge candles, hanging on the walls, to prove to all how many have been healed by "Mother Mary." However, the Catholic church has made the statement that there have been very few healings recognized by the official doctors of the Vatican.

In the front of the great church edifice above the grotto, there is a huge picture of The Virgin Mary depicted as recorded in Revelation 12:1, *"clothed with the sun, and the moon under her feet, and upon her head a crown of twelve stars."* There people worship the "Virgin," the "Mother of God." This is nothing less than idolatry and paganism. Thousands who crowd that place seeking healing must return home disillusioned and still living in darkness. Hundreds who go there die either coming or going, whether it be in bus or car accidents.

We have now seen the unusual growth of the mustard seed and we cannot help but compare this parable to the Church of Pergamos found in the book of Revelation chapter 2. In fact, all the parables follow, to a certain extent, John's description of the church age revealed through the Spirit's message to the churches. We shall look now to what extent this growth will develop and for that we must look at the following parable.

5

The Leaven

> Another parable spake he unto them; The Kingdom of
> heaven is like unto leaven, which a woman took, and hid in
> three measures of meal, till the whole was leavened.
> (Matthew 13:33)

Once again we find no explanation of the parable. Now for the first time, it is not a question of a "man" sowing seed, but of a "woman" making bread.

The explanation one hears more often than any other of this parable is that the Gospel, that works like leaven, will so permeate the world's poplulation that finally everyone will be saved. Nothing could be farther from the truth.

Scripture is its best commentary and we shall look first at what the Bible says about leaven in other passages. Let it be said that throughout all Scripture, leaven stands for evil and not for good. In Exodus 12:15 *"Seven days shall ye eat unleavened bread; even the first day ye shall put away leaven out of your houses: for whosoever eateth leavened bread from the first day until the seventh day, that soul shall be cut off from Israel."* Then we read again in the same book in the same chapter, verse 19, *"....for whosoever eateth that which is leavened, even that soul shall be cut off from the congregation of Israel, whether he be a stranger, or born in the land."*

In the New Testament, we find that the meaning of the word "leaven" still stands for that which is evil. In Matthew 16:6 *"Then Jesus said unto them, Take heed and beware of the **leaven** of the Pharisees* *and of the Sadducees.*"And again in verse 11, "*How is it that ye do not understand that I spake it not to you concerning bread, that ye should beware of the leaven of the Pharisees and of the Sadducees?*"

Even in Paul's Epistles we see the same meaning given to leaven where we read in 1 Corinthians 5:6–8 "*Your glorying is not good, Know ye not that a little leaven leaveneth the whole lump? Purge out therefore the old leaven, that ye may be a new lump, as ye are unleavened. For even Christ our passover is sacrificed for us: Therefore let us keep the feast, not with old leaven, neither with the leaven of malice and wickedness; but with the unleavened bread of sincerity and truth.*" It is in these verses that the Apostle Paul makes it very clear that leaven is wickedness.

How can a word carry the same thought throughout all Scripture, and all of a sudden, without any other explanation, change its meaning? How can anyone take himself to be a teacher of the Bible and so neglect to study it? Leaven has always meant evil and in this parable we are studying, the word *leaven* still has the same bad connotation. Secondly, the message of Christ does not work like leaven in the world. Leaven (yeast) works by the process of contamination until the whole loaf is raised. I know, I used to make bread and sell it. One must wait till the leaven does its job by causing the loaf to "rise" before it can be put in the oven. Sin works like yeast. This is why Paul was saying to put all leaven out of our lives and churches. If we don't act and act quickly, sin will completely dominate us and destroy a whole assembly of believers.

How we wish, in some way, when trying to evangelize, that the Gospel would work like leaven. We could just contact someone in a far off land, explain the Gospel to him, leave him a Bible, and just sit and wait till that whole country was totally evangelized and every soul was in the Kingdom of God. Nothing to do but sit and wait—or play golf! Alas, it doesn't work that way. Souls are often won through tears and sometimes blood. The world can only be evangelized through much sacrifice and work. Many missionaries bury their loved ones on the field before ever returning home after a lifetime struggling to win souls and build churches. No, countries are not won by simply sitting and watching the "leaven" do its work.

The Lord didn't need to explain the "woman" either, for in Zechariah we see a similar parable in chapter 5, verses 5–7 *"Then the angel that talked with me went forth, and said unto me, Lift up now thine eyes, and see what is this that goeth forth. And I said What is it? And he said...this is a woman that sitteth in the midst of the ephah."* Then in the following verse the Lord gives the explanation of the woman, *"And He said,* **This is wickedness**. *And he cast it into the midst of the ephah; and he cast the weight of lead upon the mouth thereof."*

The Final Results of the Leaven

Then how are we to interpret this? As we said before, this is a prophetic parable and the Lord used it to show to what extent His message would be distorted and corrupted: *till the whole world be leavened*. When the true Church, the salt of the earth, shall be taken Home, all churches will be united into one great world religion—a one-world church. Since we saw that the woman in Revelation 17 is understood to be the Vatican at Rome, we can conclude that all the other religions, especially those of the western world, shall be gathered into this one-world church led by the Pope. Almost weekly we are informed of more meetings of dialogue between Protestants and Catholics with a deep desire on their part to see all barriers (those that have existed through the centuries) fall at last before the feet of those who today are seeking peace and reconciliation. We are told to consider only that which unites and not that which divides.

More and more, we hear those who say that we must answer our Lord's prayer when He asked His Father in John 17:21, *"That they all may be one; as thou, Father, art in me, and I in thee, that they also may be one in us: that the world may believe that thou hast sent me."* The world needs to see a united church and not one that is fractured into a hundred different groups and denominations. This is needed so that the world will be able to believe. Let us answer our "Lord's prayer," is what we hear coming from various denominations as well as from the lips of renowned leaders in the Evangelical movement. What blasphemy!

God Himself United the Church

God did not wait 2000 years to answer His Son's prayer - and especially not by liberal preachers, many of whom are not even saved! The answer to our Lord's prayer came directly from heaven just a little more than a month after He prayed. On the day of Pentecost, the Church came into being and Christ's prayer was answered. At that very moment the believers became one, united to one another and united to Christ. *"For by one Spirit are we all baptized into one body, whether we be Jews or Gentiles, whether we be bond or free; and have been all made to drink into one Spirit."* (1 Corinthians 12:13) On that same day, those disciples, designated by our Lord as the "good seed," were blended into one **unleavened loaf.** The members of the true church form the mystical "body" of the Lord Himself. We are one with Him and one before the world. We are to strive to keep the unity of the faith and show to the world what Christ can do through sinners saved by grace through faith.

Peter Opens the Door to the Jews

No one making a thorough study of the Word of God can deny that the Church was born on the day of Pentecost. We read nowhere in the Scriptures that the Church had a second beginning as some are teaching today. However, the church that was born that day did not encompass what it does today. When Peter preached that great message and three thousand souls came to Christ, all who were saved and baptized that day were Jews. It was a totally Jewish church that began on the day of Pentecost.

Before Christ died, He gave the keys of the church to Peter. Matthew 16:18–19 *"And I say also unto thee, That thou art Peter, and upon this rock I will build my church* (Christ didn't mean He was going to build His Church on the foundation of Peter, but on Himself. This is clearly brought out by Peter himself in his first Epistle, where he says, in chapter 2:6–7 *"Wherefore also it is contained in the scripture, Behold, I lay in Sion a chief corner stone, elect, precious: and he that believeth on him shall not be confounded. Unto you therefore which believe He is precious: but unto them which be disobedient, the stone which the builders disallowed, the same is made the head of the corner."* It is evident here that Peter was talking about Christ and not about himself); *and the gates of hell shall not prevail against it. And I will give unto thee the keys of the kingdom of heaven."*

Peter, with those keys, opened the door to the Jewish people on the day of Pentecost, but the door was not yet opened to everyone. Just before ascending into heaven, Christ said to those about Him, *"But ye shall receive power, after that the Holy Ghost is come upon you: and ye shall be witnesses unto me both in Jerusalm, and in all Judaea, and in Samaria, and unto the uttermost part of the earth."* (Acts 1:8) Peter still had to open the door to the Samaritans and to the Gentiles.

Peter Opens the Door to the Samaritans

In Acts 8, we read about Philip going down to the city of Samaria where he preached Christ unto them. We read in verse 6, *"And the people with one accord gave heed unto those things which Philip spake, hearing and seeing the miracles which he did."* Philip was witnessing a revival in that place. The news of what was happening reached Jerusalem and the ears of the Apostles. *"Now when the apostles which were at Jerusalem heard that Samaria had received the word of God, they sent unto them Peter and John: Who, when they were come down, prayed for them, that they might receive the Holy Ghost: (For as yet he was fallen upon none of them: only they were baptized in the name of the Lord Jesus.) Then laid they their hands on them, and they received the Holy Ghost."* (Acts 8:14–17)

Now the door was opened to the Samaritans. The Samaritans were part Jewish and part Assyrian as a result of the Assyrian invasion that had taken place during the reign of Hoshea over Israel as recorded in 2 Kings 17. The Jews in Judaea would have nothing to do with them and would not go through their country when traveling from Jerusalem to Galilee.

Peter Opens the Door to the Gentiles

However, our Lord said to go *"to the uttermost part of the earth."* The door was now opened to the Jews and the Samaritans, but it still remained closed to the Gentiles. Then one day God revealed to Peter in a vision that he was not to consider any man impure. When Peter arrived at the home of Cornelius in Caesarea, as recorded in Acts 10, God had prepared his servant for this ordeal. Peter was such a strict Jew that he would have never imagined himself going into the house of a Gentile if the Lord had not given him this vision to prepare him for that historic moment. Many of God's children today are not always ready to go certain places or undertake certain things that God has laid on their hearts, but He has a way of making them "*ready.*" If the Lord is laying something on your heart, do it, don't wait till He "makes you ready to go;" for waiting or refusing to do His will might cost you more than you ever imagined.

We read in verse 44 of that wonderful 10th chapter of Acts, *"While Peter yet spake these words, the Holy Ghost fell on all them which heard the word."* And now the door is opened to everyone. From henceforth the message to everyone is, *"And the Spirit and the bride say, Come. And let him that heareth say, Come. And let him that is athirst come. And whosoever will, let him take the water of life freely."* (Revelation 22:17) Christ didn't die for a strict "elite" alone, but for "whosoever will." The invitation to be saved for eternity is open to everyone.

Christ began His ministry by taking up the same refrain as that of John the Baptist, by saying, *"Repent ye: for the kingdom of heaven is at hand."* (Matthew 3:2) The Kingdom of Heaven was at hand because the King was there in their midst. Had the Jews accepted Him as their Messiah and King, the church would have never been born. But no, they cried out, "Crucify Him" and because of that, they cut themselves off from the blessed Kingdom Age prophesied so often in the Old Testament—isn't that right?—no it's WRONG!

Christ's death was prophesied throughout the pages of the Old Testament. We cannot help but see how clearly His sufferings are portrayed in Psalm 22 and in Isaiah 53 as well as in other books. Christ came to give His life as a ransom for sin. John the Baptist said, *"Behold the Lamb of God."* The Jewish people who heard him say those words knew that a "lamb" was the designated animal for the sacrifice for sins. This is exactly what Peter was saying in his message on the day of Pentecost, *"Him, being delivered by the **determinate counsel and foreknowledege of God**, ye have taken, and by wicked hands have crucified and slain."* (Acts 2:23)

Paul realized that the cross was in God's heart from all eternity and Christ's death was predestinated and this is why he could write, *"But when the **fulness of the time was come**, God sent forth his Son, made of a woman, made under the law, To redeem them that were under the law, that we might receive the adoption of sons."* (Galatians 4:4–5) Christ came at a fixed time to accomplish God's plan. Jesus came to die and not to set up His earthly Kingdom. Nevertheless, our Lord was not offering the Jews, of His day, something He was not willing to give them at that time. But because He is omniscient, knowing the end from the beginning, He could offer them the Kingdom at that time, knowing full well they would refuse it and choose rather to crucify Him as was predicted in the Scriptures.

It is true that the Jewish people played a great role in Christ's death, but so did the Romans—and so did we! We all had a part in nailing Christ to the cross. We have all sinned and need a Saviour. He came to die for us all. God did not refuse the Kingdom to the Jews because they refused to accept Christ as their Messiah or because they cried out "crucify Him." We must never forget He came expressly to be crucified. This was in the plan of God from the beginning. Then what is the real reason the Jews couldn't have their Kingdom at that time if it wasn't because they refused their Messiah and asked Pilate to crucify Him? We must look farther to find the answer.

There came a day, after the crucifixion, after Christ's burial and resurrection, after the miracles of Pentecost, after the diffusion of the Holy Spirit, after the wonderful preaching of Peter, after the salvation of more than 3,000 souls and even after the miracle that took place at the Temple where Peter and John, in the Name of Christ, healed an impotent beggar who had never walked a day in his life, Peter ONCE AGAIN offered the Jewish people the Kingdom of Heaven.

This incident took place after a miraculous healing on the part of Peter and John. We read in Acts 3:6–8, *"Then Peter said, Silver and gold have I none; but such as I have give I thee: In the name of Jesus Christ of Nazareth rise up and walk. And he took him by the right hand,*

and lifted him up: and immediately his feet and ankle bones received strength. And he leaping up stood, and walked, and entered with them into the temple, walking, and leaping, and praising God."

We also read that *"all the people saw him walking and praising God."* Everything that had happened to Christ, everything that took place at Pentecost, this miracle performed in the name of Christ, all took place in Jerusalem before the eyes of everyone. All the common people knew about these events as well as those in authority. Caiaphas, the High Priest, knew about Christ, for he was the one who sat in judgment when the Son of God was brought before him. All the other priests knew about Him because they had taken counsel as to how to kill Him, and then offered Judas money to betray Him. I'm saying all this because of what follows after the healing of this beggar.

We come now to a very important passage of Scripture that is often overlooked. When the crowds saw what had happened to the impotent man who was now jumping and praising God, they all ran to where Peter and John were standing. It is there that Peter gives the Jewish people a final opportunity to repent and enter into the Kingdom Age, promised by the prophets in the past.

After telling them that they had denied the Prince of Life and had chosen a murderer to be released to them, he said that they had done this in ignorance, and that all the events that had preceded this moment had been related by the prophets. The Cross as well as the Resurrection were now history.

It was then Peter said, *"Repent ye therefore, and be converted, that your sins may be blotted out, when **the times of refreshing shall come from the presence of the Lord; And he shall send Jesus Christ,** which before was preached unto you: Whom the heaven must receive until the times of restitution of all things, which God hath spoken by the mouth of all his holy prophets since the world began."* (Acts 3:19-21) Here Peter gives the Jewish people their last chance to have the Kingdom at that time. He promised them that if they would repent, God would send back Jesus and would give them those wonderful "times of refreshing" for which they had been waiting for so many years. The Millennium would have been upon them.

And what was their response to this astounding offer? They categorically refused it and put Peter and John in prison. *"And as*

*they spake unto the people, the priests, and the captain of the temple, and
the Sadducees, came upon them, Being grieved that they taught the people,
and preached through Jesus the resurrection from the dead. And they laid
hands on them, and put them in hold unto the next day: for it was now
eventide.* "(Acts 4:1-3) This was the national response of Israel given
by their leaders to Peter's immediate offer of the Kingdom of
Heaven. Christ's crucifixion was set from all eternity and written
in the Bible, but the rejection of the Kingdom by the leaders of
Israel after Pentecost *wasn't* predicted. They had witnessed His
miracles as well as those performed by His disciples after the de-
scent of the Holy Spirit. However, in spite of all this, they gave
their definite reply to God's last offer—and it was NO. They officially refused the Kingdom. This was a deliberate, thought-through
decision that cost them the Millennium at that time. For them to
have accepted Peter's offer would have meant to everyone that
they had falsely accused and crucified the Lord. It would have
been an open declaration that what they did was wrong—and how
could they ever admit that?

Their pride wouldn't permit them to repent and this *pride* cost
them the Kingdom. They preferred, rather, to persecute those who
did believe that Christ was the Messiah. Think of how many today
refuse to come to Christ for eternal life simply because to do so
would mean to declare publicly that they had been wrong up to now.
For some it would mean denying the religion they have followed for
so many years, to others it would mean leaving *certain friends.* Pride
stands as a door that keeps millions from coming to the cross.

As we have said previously, the Church was born on the day
of Pentecost. The Church only had one beginning, but the Samaritans and Gentiles were added to it afterwards. Here, however, we
see that the great CHURCH AGE began after Peter's offer in Acts
3. The Church, *as we know it today*, didn't begin until after that
cold, national response of Israel to Peter's pleadings. If at that time,
Israel had repented and recognized that Jesus was God's Son manifested in the flesh, there would have been no Church Age! God
would have sent Christ back to earth and His earthly reign would
have begun just as Peter promised them.

God's promises in the Old Testament never included the Gentiles as part of the Church. This was something revealed to Paul

and the other Apostles later after the door had been opened to the Gentiles by Peter. Paul refers to the blessed truth of Jews and Gentiles being united in one body as having been "hid in God" through those former years and is only now revealed to the Apostles as present church doctrine. *"Whereby, when ye read, ye may understand my knowledge in the mystery of Christ) Which in other ages was not made known unto the sons of men, as it is now revealed unto his holy apostles and prophets by the Spirit; That the Gentiles should be fellow-heirs, and of the same body, and partakers of his promise in Christ by the gospel: Whereof I was made a minister, according to the gift of the grace of God given unto me by the effectual working of his power."* (Ephesians 3:4–7)

God's great mystery, kept secret throughout the ages, is His Church. Yes, we know we will be joint-heirs with Christ to share all His riches, we know that we are the "Bride" of Christ, we know we will be like Him, we know we shall dwell with Him throughout eternity, but when all this is said, we still cannot comprehend what it really means to be part of "His Church." God still has "great secrets" hidden in Himself that will not be revealed to us until we see Him face to face.

6

The Hidden Treasure

Again, the kingdom of heaven is like unto treasure hid in a
field; the which when a man hath found, he hideth, and for
joy thereof goeth and selleth all that he hath, and buyeth
that field. Matthew 13:44

Whether it was in Czechoslovakia shortly after World War II,
or in France in the following years, or visiting churches around
America, I heard the same explanation of this parable. "The interpretation is very clear and simple," a preacher would say, and
then go on to expound it by pointing out that the "treasure" cannot
be anything else, but our precious Lord Himself. He is a "treasure" beyond anything a man could ever imagine or hope to possess. Everyone must be ready to "sell all" to purchase this inesti-
mable treasure. One must be ready to give up worldly pleasures,
be engaged in a local church and ready to make any necessary
sacrifices. Only in this way may a man have what it will take to
purchase such a wonderful treasure.

However, a closer examination of this parable leads us to an
altogether different interpretation. First of all, no man can ever
purchase Christ or salvation. No amount of work, suffering or
clean living will ever earn a man's way into Glory. Nothing that
comes from man has any purchasing value at the store of heaven.
It is not what we do that brings salvation, but what Christ has
already done. We are saved by faith and not by works. This is the
whole message of the New Testament.

Then too, when a man is truly saved, he does not go out and bury his new-found treasure, as we see in this parable, but rather he is to let his light so shine before men that others will come to the Truth.

Since Christ gave no explanation to this parable, we must refer to what we learned in the study of the first two parables. We learned that the "man" in them is our Lord. He is the One who finds the treasure, and it is He, who after purchasing it, buries it in a field. We also learned that the "field" is the world.

Building on Truths We Know

When studying a parable, one must build his exegesis on things already revealed in former ones, in order to try to discover the meaning of the things which have not as yet been explained. What we already know, is that our Lord is the One who found the treasure and then hid it in the world. We know, too, that He sold all that He had to purchase the world. Paul explained what it meant for Christ to "sell all" to purchase our salvation in his letter to the church in Philippi, chapter 2:5–8, *"Let this mind be in you, which was also in Christ Jesus: Who, being in the form of God, thought it not robbery to be equal with God: But made himself of no reputation, and took upon him the form of a servant, and was made in the likeness of men: And being found in fashion as a man, he humbled himself, and became obedient unto death, even the death of the cross."* Our Lord truly sold everything when he left heaven's glory, to be counted as an impostor, to be spit upon, beaten, crowned with thorns and nailed to a tree. Only He, being the perfect Son of God, could ever pay for the sins of the whole world as we read in 1 John 2:2, *"And he is the propitiation for our sins: and not for our's only, but also for the sins of the whole world."*

What is the Treasure?

There remains an important element in this parable that has not as yet been explained–*the "treasure itself."* The Lord didn't say that the *church* is like unto a treasure. Neither did He say that the *Kingdom of Heaven* is like unto a treasure. What He said

was, "the Kingdom of Heaven is like a *treasure hid in a field.*"
We must take the whole phrase if we are to understand it. Let
us remind ourselves that Christ was not giving His disciples
Church doctrine. Throughout the whole Gospel of Matthew,
which was addressed primarily to the Jewish people, He was
teaching and was referring to them in this parable as "a treasure." This coincides with what our Lord said to His twelve
disciples, *"...Go not into the way of the Gentiles, and into any city
of the Samaritans enter ye not: But go rather to the lost sheep of the
house of Israel."* (Matthew 10:5–6) We read, too, in John 1:11–
12: *"He came unto His own* (the Jewish people)*, and His own
received him not. But as many as received him, to them gave he power
to become the sons of God, even to them that believe on his name."* It
was only after "His own" refused Him that the message was
given to the whole world.

Let us look carefully once more at what Christ said in this
parable. The treasure that our Lord found was hidden somewhere
in the world. Then when He finds it, He hides it somewhere else in
the world. Where was the treasure "hid" when Christ found it.
The Jewish people were already scattered to several different countries, but they were mainly in the land of Israel, the center of the
world. The land of Israel is known to be virtually in the center of
the earth mass. God wanted His people to be a witness to the world
of His sovereignty over the nations and His mighty power to save
and to deliver.

The children of Israel were still in the Land during our
Lord's ministry, but we must remember that this is a prophetic
parable. We must try to see what Christ was revealing to His
disciples. His children would not be left in the Land after His
death, the Roman armies would destroy the Temple and the
Jews would be dispersed throughout the world. Christ would
again hide them, but now they would be hidden throughout the
entire world, swallowed up by the Gentile nations. I like to
think of the people of Israel being hid in God's Hand during all
those years of their dispersion, even as we, who know the Lord
today, are held in His hand. *"And I give unto them eternal life; and
they shall never perish, neither shall any man pluck them out of my
hand."* (John 10:28)

The Kingdom of Heaven can best be defined as that period of time preceeding Christ's coming in glory. It does embrace Christendom, but particularly singles out the Tribulation period that immediately preceeds the Millennium.

This parable was given to comfort the hearts of His people because He would not only "sell all that He had" to purchase them, but would keep them through to the end of this age. This is why we see Him having such "joy" when He sells all to purchase them—*and us.*

7

The Pearl

Again, the kingdom of heaven is like unto a merchant man,
seeking goodly pearls: Who, when he had found one pearl
of great price, went and sold all that he had, and bought it.
Matthew 13:45–46

Here again we see our Lord selling "all that He had," but this
time it is to buy a "Pearl of Great Price." We see Him first of all
"seeking" goodly pearls. Our Lord is forever seeking out those
who are lost. In the wonderful parable found in Luke 15, we see
Him represented by someone seeking a lost sheep, a lost coin and
finally a lost son. Our Lord never tires of seeking lost sinners. Oh,
that Christians, the world over, would have that same compassion
for those who are still without Christ and without hope. Chrstians
today do not realize the horror of Hell and the urgency to win
souls to Christ.

The parable greatly resembles the former one, even to the
extent that it could simply mean that the Lord was emphasizing in
different words what he previously had stated.

The Pearl is not the Lord

We do now know that the Pearl of Great Price is not the Lord
because we do not sell all we have to buy Christ. We don't have
enough money, and furthermore, Christ isn't for sale! Many commentaries on this parable declare that the Pearl can only be the

Chruch for whom Christ died. Certainly this is a beautiful image and it is true that Christ "paid it all" to purchase it. Besides this, a pearl is the result of much suffering as the oyster continually tries to cover a grain of sand that has made its way into the shell. Not only did Christ have to suffer terrible agony on the cross, but the true Church also has suffered through the centuries in the development of this Pearl as Paul stated in Colossians 1:24, *"Who now rejoice in my sufferings for you, and fill up that which is behind of the afflictions of Christ in my flesh for his body's sake, which is the church."* Paul was not saying that Christ didn't pay the total price for our redemption and that he, Paul, had to also suffer to complete Christ's work on the cross. Rather, he was saying that he was suffering to complete the building of the Church. There are still servants of God who are suffering to bring in the last souls before the Trump of God sounds.

Though the Pearl makes a beautiful picture of the Church in so many ways, yet the Pearl of Great Price is not the Church. Christ said that the "Kingdom of Heaven" is like a pearl of great price. He didn't say that the Church is the pearl. We must constantly remember that the Kingdom of Heaven is not the Church. We do so want to put ourselves into everything we read in the Bible, (and this is the way it should be most of the time) and because of that, it is hard to come to the reality that though all the Word is for us, all the Bible does not apply directly to us. Here is definitely a case in point.

If the Pearl is not Christ, nor the Church, what is it? In the previous parable we found that the Kingdom of Heaven was compared to a Treasure hidden in a field, even as Israel was hidden in the world. Once again it is a question of the Kingdom of Heaven but this time it is compared to a Pearl of Great Price and must have something to do with Israel again, but what?

God revealed to Joel what would happen in the Day of the Lord, the day when Christ will return to judge the world. In chapter 2:30–32 *"And I will shew wonders in the heavens and in the earth, blood, and fire, and pillars of smoke. The sun shall be turned into darkness, and the moon into blood, before the great and the terrible day of the LORD come. And it shall come to pass, that whosoever shall call on the name of the LORD shall be delivered: for in mount Zion and in Jerusalem* *shall be deliverance, as the LORD hath said, and in the **remnant** whom the Lord shall call."*

The Remnant

There we have it. The Pearl of Great Price is that precious *remnant* that will turn to the Lord when He descends to defend Jerusalem. Then will come to pass that wonderful moment we read about in Zechariah 12:10, *"And I will pour upon the house of David, and upon the inhabitants of Jerusalem, the spirit of grace and of supplications: and they shall look upon me whom they have pierced, and they shall mourn for him, as one mourneth for his only son, and shall be in bitterness for him, as one that is in biterness for his firstborn."*

The Apostle Paul also wrote about this great day when he said, *"And so **all Israel shall be saved**: as it is written, There shall come out of Sion the Deliverer, and shall turn away ungodliness from Jacob: For this is my covenant unto them, when I shall take away their sins."* (Romans 11:26–27) The Godly remnant must go through the furnace heated by the wrath of the Antichrist and Satan. It shall be a trial by fire. But at the moment when it looks as if the Antichrist will destroy all the remaining Jews in Israel, Christ shall appear and all those in Israel who are still alive, will fall on their faces and repent in the dust as they see Him whom they pierced. And thus, all Israel (the faithful *remnant*) shall be saved in a day. We see now that the "remnant" is the Pearl of Great Price.

It is hard to believe that the Jews will again be persecuted after having been chased from country to country for the past 2000 years. There is hardly a country in the world that has not persecuted God's earthly people. We cannot help but think of what Moses predicted 3,500 years ago would happen to the children of Israel if they neglected God and forgot His commandments, *"In the morning thou shalt say, Would God it were even! and at even thou shalt say, Would God it were morning!"* (Deuteronomy 28:67) Thus it has been throughout this whole church age and especially was it true in the horrible days of the Holocaust. Even now they are not living in peace in their own land, but the situation will only become worse until the King of Peace comes to restore the Millennial rest in the Land.

8

The Drag Net

Again, the kingdom of heaven is like unto a net, that was cast into the sea, and gathered of every kind: Which, when it was full, they drew to shore, and sat down, and gathered the good into vessels, but cast the bad away. So shall it be at the end of the world: the angels shall come forth, and sever the wicked from among the just, And shall cast them into the furnace of fire: there shall be wailing and gnashing of teeth. Matthew 13: 47–50

What has never failed to amuse me is the response of the disciples to Christ's question when He asked them if they had understood all the truths of these parables. *"Jesus saith unto them, Have ye understood all these things? They say unto him, Yea, Lord."* (Matthew 13:51) They truly believed that they had grasped all Christ was teaching in those "mystery parables" but we, after nearly 2000 years, have still not fathomed the depths. The reason the disciples thought they had understood everything is the same reason that Christians today feel they have understood them—it is because they look so simple on the surface. We so readily understand every word that it just doesn't seem possible that we could have missed something along the way. All the parables were based on things the people had done for centuries, sowing seed, making bread, fishing with nets—of course they believed that they had understood everything!

Now we face the last parable of this chapter. It reserves for us more questions to answer and problems to solve. There is no explanation given by our Lord, so we must, by comparing Scripture with Scripture, find the hidden meanings therein.

We have already seen that the "sea" represents the world when we studied the Antichrist coming out of the sea. Then there is a "net" that is cast into this sea and this "net cast into the sea" represents the Kingdom of Heaven at the "end of the world." This expression, "the end of the world" can also be translated, the "end of this age," which will culminate at the return of our Lord in glory.

What is the Net?

What is the "net?" Since the Lord gave no explanation of it, we can only come to the conclusion that this time "Christ's message" which will eventually become Christendom, embracing all sorts of false doctrines, is now called the "net." Christendom is cast into the waters of the world and will catch both good and bad fish. We were told in the second parable where Satan sowed tares among the good seed, that our Lord said they should grow together "until the harvest." Christ is now comparing the "harvest" to a "catch of fish" when He returns. The two parables are almost identical. In the explanation of the "Tares" we read in verses 40 through 42 *"As therefore the tares are gathered and burned in the fire; so shall it be in the end of this world. The Son of man shall send forth his angels, and they shall gather out of his kingdom all things that offend, and them which do iniquity; And shall cast them into a furnace of fire: there shall be wailing and gnashing of teeth."*

In both of these parables we see angels coming forth to separate the good from the bad. They cast the bad "into a furnace of fire" in the parable of the Tares and we find exactly the same words in the parable of the Net "And shall cast them into the furnace of fire."

So shall it be at the coming of our Lord in glory. "One shall be taken and the other left." One shall be cast into the fire of hell and the other left to enter into the Millennial Period. This is Christ's teaching throughout the parables in Matthew.

We have seen that these two parables are very similar, but Christ was not repeating Himself. There is something very important added to this parable which is not in the one about the Tares. When a net is cast it doesn't catch all the fish in the sea. All the "fish" in the sea will *not* be caught in the net of Christendom. Though it is said that there are now one billion people considered to be "Christians," this is far from embracing the six billion that comprise the population of the planet.

Those who will be judged so severely, at the coming of the Lord, and cast immediately into hell, will be those who knew about Him, claimed to belong to Him, but were not born again. They belonged to Christendom, but were not true children of God. The good "fish" will be those who never accepted the "mark of the Beast" and remained faithful to God throughout the Tribulation Period. How they managed to escape receiving the "mark" or how they lived during those years without being able to buy or sell is not revealed in the Bible. All we know is that the angels will separate the good from the bad, and that when Christ returns in glory, "one shall be taken (in judgment) and the other left to go into the Millennium. Therefore we can only accept that there will be some "good fish" at the end of the Tribulation Period.

The millions who were never "caught by the net" and had never embraced Christianity, will be judged at the Judgement of the Nations. Every little detail of all that will happen is not revealed in the Word, but God did reveal all we need to know at this present time. He especially made salvation so clear that even a wayfaring man should not err therein. Prophecy must never take first place in the life of any believer. We are called to live holy lives and to make Christ known. We are to evangelize the unsaved, baptize and disciple the new believers and bring them into a Bible-believing church where they can be fed and encouraged.

9

The Ten Virgins

Then shall the kingdom of heaven be likened unto ten virgins, which took their lamps, and went forth to meet the bridegroom. And five of them were wise, and five were foolish. They that were foolish took their lamps, and took no oil with them: But the wise took oil in their vessels with their lamps. While the bridegroom tarried, they all slumbered and slept. And at midnight there was a cry made, Behold, the bridegroom cometh; go ye out to meet him. Then all those virgins arose, and trimmed their lamps. And the foolish said unto the wise, Give us of your oil; for our lamps are gone out. But the wise answered, saying, Not so; lest there be not enough for us and you: but go ye rather to them that sell, and buy for yourselves. And while they went to buy, the bridegroom came; and they that were ready went in with him to the marriage: and the door was shut. Afterward came also the other virgins, saying, Lord, Lord, open to us. But he answered and said, Verily I say unto you, I know you not. Watch therefore, for ye know neither the day nor the hour wherein the Son of man cometh. (Matthew 25:1-13)

We felt that this parable should be included in this book because it is often misinterpreted and so frequently used as an argument to prove one can lose his salvation. It is a beautiful parable and adds much to the ones we have already studied since it begins with the same words, "Then shall the kingdom of heaven be likened unto..."

The Ten Virgins Resembled Each Other

What we need to notice first of all, is how greatly the ten virgins resemble each other. As a starter, we can see that all ten were virgins. By saying this, we must conclude that all of them were pure in God's eyes—in other words, all had been washed by the blood of Christ since no one is pure in His eyes on the basis of his own personal worthiness. God has said that *"all have sinned, and come short of the glory of God;"* (Romans 3:23) and to prove that all have sinned, Paul says we all die. Not one of the greatest of all saints, since the days of Adam, has continued living till this day as a proof they had never sinned. We read in Romains 5:12, *"Wherefore, as by one man sin entered into the world, and death by sin; and so death passed upon all men, for all have sinned."* Every grave and every tombstone cries out to the whole world that every man is a sinner. Only those who have been to Calvary and found salvation through Christ's blood can ever be considered pure in His eyes.

Not only were all ten virgins pure, all ten of them *"went forth to meet the bridegroom."* In other words, all were waiting for Christ. They were not forgetful of His promise to return. They were not out in the world amusing themselves. None had given up the hope of His coming. How we wish this could be said of all God's children today. Most believers are living for themselves and their immediate family. They are profiting from the wave of prosperity in which the western world has been bathing now for nearly 40 years. "Buy now and pay later" has encouraged people to live far beyond their means and Christians are not exempt from this temptation.

Just before his execution, in his second letter to Timothy chapter 4, verse 8, the Apostle Paul wrote, *"Henceforth there is laid up for me a crown of righteousness, which the Lord, the righteous judge, shall give me at that day: and not to me only, but unto all them also that love his appearing."* As a young believer I concluded that of all the crowns that are promised to Christians, this certainly would be the easiest of them all to acquire. Certainly it is much easier than trying to win souls (1 Thessalonians 2:19–20), or being faithful in feeding the flock (1 Peter 5:4),and definitely far easier than martyrdom (Revelation 2:10).

With the passing of time, I took a whole different view of this crown. "Loving His appearing" involves more than singing about it from time to time on Sunday morning. It means more than not to love the world and its pleasures or being faithful to one's wife. It goes much farther than that. It is impossible to "love His appearing" and still be absent from prayer meetings and Bible studies, or not be fully engaged in a local church, or never trying to win a soul to Christ. No, I'm not saying it is harder to win this crown than the one the martyrs will be handed at the appearing of Christ, but there will be many fewer receiving this crown, than it might seem at first glance. We should all do our best, not to strive to win this crown or one of the others, but we should give our all and do our very best to serve our Lord out of love for Him who held nothing back to save us.

Then we notice in this parable, that all of their lamps were burning brightly. We know this to be true because even in the case of the foolish virgins, their lamps were burning as were those of the wise virgins. How do we know this? Because it says in verse 8, "Give us of your oil; for our lamps are gone out." (which should be translated "going out" as brought to our attention in the margin of most King James Bibles) and translated as such in our French version. Lamps cannot be "going out" unless they are burning at the time.

Because all lamps were burning, all ten virgins had *oil.* Kings, priests and prophets were all anointed with oil in the Old Testament as a figure of being anointed with the Holy Spirit. Oil became the symbol of the Holy Spirit. This parable is not the exception to the rule. All ten virgins had a lamp and all ten virgins had oil. In other words, the Lord is telling us that all of them had the Holy Spirit and were therefore all Children of God.

Another resemblance between the ten is found in the fact that all ten "were sleeping" when the call rang out that the Bridegroom was coming. It's not the greatest sin to be asleep when the Lord comes, as seen in this parable, but how much better it would have been if all had been awake. After giving this parable, Christ said to His disciples, *"Watch therefore, for ye know neither the day nor the hour wherein the Son of man cometh."* (verse 13) All of Christ's disciples were sleeping in the Garden of Gethsemane on that unforgettable evening when he needed their help as never before. Only one was not sleeping; he was out betraying the Son of God for thirty pieces of silver! What a picture that makes of the greater part of the church today—most everyone is asleep except those who are betraying Christ through their evident apostasy.

The Only Difference Between the Ten Virgins

Now that we have seen how all ten virgins resembled each other, we must look at why God called five of them wise and the others foolish. It can be summed up in one short phrase, *"took no oil with them"* (verse 3) and also in verse 8, *"Give us of your oil."* We have already seen that all ten had oil because all their lamps were burning when the call came that the Bridegroom was coming. What is the secret?

In the days of our Lord, people carried little lamps in the palms of their hands to light their paths as they walked around in the dark. If they were going some distance and figured the oil in their lamps would not be sufficient for the time they would be out, they simply took a little pitcher of oil (about three inches high) as a supplement, just in case. I have held in my hands both a little lamp as well as the little vase they used for the extra oil they needed. The foolish virgins simply did not take along that little pitcher in case they didn't have enough oil in their lamps.

At the time of a wedding in those days, the friends of the bridegroom waited for him to come because the wedding could not take place before his arrival. The greater the importance of the bridegroom, the longer he waited before coming to the wedding. The foolish virgins didn't realize the greatness of this Bridegroom for whom they were waiting. Of course, they wouldn't have enough oil in their lamps to carry them through, unless they took an extra supply of oil. This is why the Lord called them "the foolish virgins." To take that little pitcher would not have burdened them down that much. It is an example of the attitude of God's people in the last days. They always want the easy way, no sacrifice and no demands. These foolish virgins should have realized the importance of the Bridegroom and should have carried an extra supply of that which represents the Holy Spirit.

Enduring to the End

What was our Lord trying to tell His disciples? Again, let us not forget that this parable begins with the words, *"Then shall the **kingdom of heaven** be likened unto ten virgins."* Christ didn't say that "then shall the **church** be likened unto ten virgins." This is not a parable addressed to the Church, but to His people and all who will be living at a certain time in history—at the time of the Great Tribulation. He was saying, in parabolic terms, what He had told them clearly in verse 13 of the preceding chapter, *"But he that shall endure unto the end, the same shall be saved."* This verse teaches that people in those days of great trial at the "end of the age" will be saved only on the *condition* that they endure to the end. In other words, it means that there will be those living during the Tribulation Age who will be saved and then, because they fail to endure to the end, will lose their salvation. This means they will accept the mark of the Beast rather than be beheaded. However, the number of those who will be martyred will be numerous for we read in Revelation 20:4, *"And I saw thrones, and they sat upon them, and judgment was given unto them: and I saw the souls of them that were beheaded for the witness of Jesus, and for the word of God, and which had not worshipped the beast, neither his image, neither had received his mark upon their foreheads, or in their hands; and they lived and reigned with Christ a thousand years."*

The "foolish virgins," by not paying attention to take an extra supply of oil to be able to endure to the end, were not ready when the Bridegroom appeared and that is why, having lost their salvation, they hear the Lord say to them in words no one would ever want to hear, *"Verily I say unto you, **I know you not**."*

Where is the Bride?

There is a very important factor here that has been over-looked by millions as they read and study this most interesting parable–something is missing! We see the Bridegroom as well as the Bridegroom's friends pictured in these "virgins" who will have endured the great Tribulation–BUT WHERE IS THE BRIDE? We do not see her simply because she will have been raptured before the Great Tribulation and will be preparing herself for the day of the wedding. The Bride of Christ is made up only of those who are saved during this most glorious period of the Grace of God known as the Church period. Even John the Baptist, the greatest of all prophets, will not be part of the Bride. In John's Gospel chapter 3, verse 29 we read: *"He that hath the bride is the bridegroom: but the **friend of the bridegroom**, which standeth and heareth him, rejoiceth greatly because of the bridegroom's voice: this my joy therefore is fulfilled."*

We, today, are living in the most wonderful of all God's dispensations–even greater than that of the future Millennium. Today we have the indwelling Holy Spirit by which we have been sealed until the Day of Redemption. We need not live in constant fear that we might lose our salvation as will those who will be saved during the Tribulation Period. Those living then will not lose their salvation simply because they coveted something or were jealous of someone, but because they accepted the Mark of the Beast to show to everyone that they, too, now carry the mark of Satan upon them. They will have openly denied their Lord.

Though this parable does not apply to us today, we should still not forget to be diligent and wait with joy for that day when we shall see our Lord face to face.

PART FOUR: CONCLUSION

Israel is in the news every day. From the moment we began writing this book until now, there have been some important incidents taking place in that land. Either a Palestinian or an Israeli has been killed, or Israeli tanks have had to roll into the "occupied territories" to restore order, or rockets have been fired from both sides and there have even been open clashes of cannon fire.

As we study the situation from a human point of view, it doesn't seem possible that the situation in the Near East can continue much longer before a full-fledged war breaks out between Israel and the surrounding countries.

We do not in any way, desire to see the events mentioned in this book take place. We have not predicted these wars—God did! We have only tried to sort them out and make it clear to everyone that these things will be happening and that we should be ready for the coming of the Lord.

Before closing, however, we do encourage each one of you to examine himself to see if he is in "the faith." It is so easy to go through life feeling that everything is just fine between us and the Lord, but there often still lacks "one thing"—the absolute assurance that one is saved. If you have any doubts whatsoever that you might not be going to heaven as you hope, now is the time to be sure of where you are going after you leave this life. Accidents happen every day. No one has a mortal accident planned in his agenda, but they come without warning.

In France, hundreds leave for vacation every summer who never return. They die climbing mountains, they drown in the sea, they are killed in automobile accidents and many simply die from heart attacks and strokes. These all make up the statistics given at the end of the summer. All of them had plans of what they were going to do when they returned home, but they never got there. Your eternal destiny is a matter of choice. Everyone chooses where he will spend Eternity.

Before France built four-lane highways throughout the country, everyone wanting to go down to the French Riviera on the Mediteranean Sea had to go on a two-lane road that passed under a railroad bridge. Someone climbed up there one night and painted in glowing white letters just one word–ETERNITY. The vacationers were so troubled as they passed under that bridge that they wrote letters to the local authorities to have that word erased. The very thought of eternity was destroying their whole vacation. No one likes to think of where he will go after death. People just want to live for today as if there were no tomorrow. When someone exhales his last breath–then eternity begins. Where will one go?–each person must answer individually. We choose where we will spend eternity.

Each of us can all ignore the warning signs God has placed along the highways of life, but by doing so, one seals his own destiny. Thousands are dying and going to Hell every day who could have gone to heaven if they had just stopped in their folly and taken the time to accept God's offer of eternal life by repenting and accepting Christ into their hearts and lives.

No one has a lease on life. No one chooses the day of his death unless he commits suicide. No one knows when he will have his last opportunity to be saved. Not only do we not know the day of our death, but we do not know the day of our Lord's return. Christ could come today. This book is to show just how close *that day* is at this time.

The greatest experience anyone can have in this life is to be saved–and know it. To enter into God's love is a blessing no one has words to express. You can never deserve this wonderful salvation. You can never buy this salvation by works or by suffering. It is a gift you can only receive by humbling yourself before the Lord and asking Him to save you on the merits of Christ's shed blood on the cross. *"For by grace are you saved through faith; and that not of yourselves:* **it is the gift of God***: Not of works, lest any man should boast. "* (Ephesians 2:8–9) If you have not already done so, accept this wonderful **gift** today.

NOTE: All emphases in the book are mine. All Scripture verses are from the King James Bible.

ABOUT THE AUTHOR: Arthur Sommerville has been a missionary in Europe for 55 years. He is now International Director of the "Society for Europe's Evangelization" (founded in 1957) and President and founder of the Paris Baptist Bible Institute. His ministry is starting Baptist churches throughout France and other countries of Europe while training young men to become pastors of these churches. He has always been deeply interested in Bible prophecies concerning the end times and has held prophetic conferences both in France and in the United States.

He was born in Chicago, Ill in 1923. His family soon moved to Oshkosh, Wisconsin where he lived until he finished high school in 1941. Knowing that the Lord was calling him to be a missionary to Europe, he left that fall for Minneapolis where he spent the next four years studying at Northwestern Bible School and Seminary.

In 1946 as soon as the war was over, he left for Europe with the hope of serving God in USSR. Not being able to obtain a visa for the land he so longed to evangelize, he ministered in Czechoslovakia near the Russian border. There he went with a translator from village to village in a troika to reach as many souls as possible with the Gospel. After learning the language, he had the joy of reaping many souls for Christ before the iron curtain fell and forced him to leave for Western Europe. For a short season he ministered in deportation camps to the refugees who had been forced by the Nazi regime to leave their respective countries.

After considering different places where he might minister, he knew that God wanted him to work in France. He, with several other missionaries, began a church in Bordeaux. From there, he and his wife Irene, went to Toulouse which became the base of their ministries for the following thirty years. It was there they began a Baptist church and a Bible School which, through the years, has graduated more than 100 students. By using permanent Gospel teams they were able to start 11 churches in France which now have as pastors those who graduated from their school.

He is presently working in Paris where he began the Central Baptist Church and brought the Bible School from Toulouse to the French capital twenty years ago. He now wants to purchase a building for this church in the heart of Paris both for the defense of the faith and to serve as a lighthouse for the lost in that city which now has 13,500,000 souls to be won to Christ.